FRASER VALLEY REGIONAL LIBRARY

D0195528

CAPTAIN PAUL WATSON

CAPTAIN PAUL WATSON

Interview with a Pirate

Lamya Essemlali with Paul Watson

FIREFLY BOOKS

A FIREFLY BOOK

Published by Firefly Books Ltd. 2013

English translation copyright © 2013 Firefly Books Ltd.

Title of the original French edition: Capitaine Paul Watson, Entretien avec un pirate © 2012 Editions Glenat, BP 177, F - 38008 Grenoble Cedex

All rights reserved. No part of this publication may be reproduced, stored in a retrieval system, or transmitted in any form or by any means, electronic, mechanical, photocopying, recording or otherwise, without the prior written permission of the Publisher.

First printing

Publisher Cataloging-in-Publication Data (U.S.)

Essemlali, Lamya
    Captain Paul Watson : interview with a pirate / Lamya Essemlali with Paul Watson.
[224] p. : ill., col. photos. ; cm.
Includes bibliographical references and index.
Summary: Paul Watson reveals to shipmate Lamya Essemlali his motivations, campaigns, dangers and successes in eco-activism.
ISBN-13: 978-1-77085-173-3 (pbk.)
1. Watson, Paul, 1950 - . 2. Conservationists -- Canada -- Biography.
I. Watson, Paul, 1950 - . II. Title.
574.0924 [B] dc23   QH31.W34A3E7846   2013

Library and Archives Canada Cataloguing in Publication

Essemlali, Lamya
    Captain Paul Watson : interview with a pirate / Lamya Essemlali with Paul Watson.
Originally published in French under title: Capitaine Paul Watson.
ISBN 978-1-77085-173-3
        1. Watson, Paul, 1950–
— Interviews. 2. Animal rights activists — Canada — Interviews. 3. Watson, Paul, 1950–
4. Animal rights movement. 5. Environmentalism. I. Watson, Paul, 1950- II. Title.
HV4716.W28E87 2013   179'.3092   C2012-906719-9

Published in the United States by
Firefly Books (U.S.) Inc.
P.O. Box 1338, Ellicott Station
Buffalo, New York 14205

Published in Canada by
Firefly Books Ltd.
50 Staples Avenue, Unit 1
Richmond Hill, Ontario L4B 0A7

Cover and Interior design
Erin R. Holmes/Soplari Design
Cover Photos
front: Jo-Anne McArthur/Sea Shepherd;
back: Triff/Shutterstock.com; Pirate ship -
Bioraven/Shutterstock.com

Printed in Canada

For the latest in Sea Shepherd news and to support the Sea Shepherd Conservation Society's activities, please visit **www.seashepherd.org**

"True human goodness, in all its purity and freedom, can come to the fore only when its recipient has no power. Mankind's true moral test, its fundamental test (which lies deeply buried from view), consists of its attitude toward those who are at its mercy: animals. And in this respect mankind has suffered a fundamental debacle, a debacle so fundamental that all others stem from it."

— Milan Kundera, *The Unbearable Lightness of Being*

ONTENTS

ACKNOWLEDGMENTS

Thank you to Paul, who showed me by example that nothing is impossible, who inspired and supported me, and who always believed in me.

Thank you to the thousands of Sea Shepherd volunteers around the world, at sea and on land. They are also a source of inspiration and hope. They are Sea Shepherd's vital breath, without which none of this would be possible.

Thank you to the thousands of people around the world who financially support the organization and enable it to maintain its fleet at sea.

And thank you to Franck Siscilia for his help with the photographs, which depict more than forty years of activism in the eventful life of Captain Paul Watson.

NTRODUCTION

In January 2005 my friend, whose brother was working with Jacques Perrin on the movie *Oceans*, which at the outset was supposed to tell the story of Paul's life, told me that Paul Watson would be coming to Paris. At that time, Sea Shepherd did not have a branch in France, and so Paul was not very well known there. But I found him intriguing; I wanted to know more about this guy who was going around sinking whaling ships. So I was really looking forward to attending the talk he would be giving that Sunday afternoon. It took place in a small room provided for the occasion by WWF France.

What I heard that afternoon marked a turning point in my life: "So, there is someone out there who thinks like me, who dares to say it and, even better, dares to do it. It *is* possible." Prior to that, I had been involved with big ecology groups, without ever feeling I belonged there and with a level of enthusiasm that was declining with every passing day. But on that Sunday afternoon, I met Captain Paul Watson and learned about the Sea Shepherd organization: the UFO of the ecology movement. When the talk was over, I went to see Paul and I was very straightforward with him. I said: "I want to help you. What can I do to help?" He answered: "If you are ready to work hard, and if you have the time, apply for a campaign at sea. But before you do, ask yourself if you are really ready to risk your life for a whale, because that is a non-negotiable condition of working with us."

The following summer, I went to Florida to meet with the *Farley Mowat*, the flagship at that time, to take part in my first campaign in the Galápagos archipelago.

In the interim, I had eagerly researched anything and everything that had been said or written about this unusual character. I read a lot of positive things about Paul — he clearly had a lot of fans — but I wasn't looking only for positive comments. I was interested in finding out who his enemies were. And I didn't have any problem finding some: "Misanthrope," "pirate," "terrorist," "guru." When I dug a little deeper into their arguments, none held up to an analysis of the real facts. All of Paul's detractors had private interests that had been more or less negatively affected by his activities. They all contributed, at least as much as Paul himself, to my decision to take the leap and join Sea Shepherd.

While my opinion about Paul's public persona was forged quickly, the same cannot be said of my opinion about the man. Some say he is arrogant, egocentric, cold, calculating, distrustful, disruptive, opportunistic, etc., and that his strongest opponents seem to be part of the "eco-intelligentsia," or the "eco-diplomatic corps." It was difficult at that time to formulate an opinion without knowing him personally.

Seven years later, after seven campaigns at sea and after accompanying him on dozens of conferences and interviews, and after about just as many days and informal evenings in his company, I am now in a position to express an opinion.

When I went aboard the *Farley Mowat* with him for my first campaign at sea, I expected him to talk about whales. But he spoke mostly about history, religion, films, poetry and music, and he would organize onboard poker tournaments. He told jokes and posed funny riddles, of which he knows hundreds. His knowledge of general culture is impressive and his uncommon ability to recall facts shows that he has vast knowledge of a lot of different topics. My friend and I gave him the nickname "WikiWatson." But Paul didn't talk about his achievements as an activist unless people brought the subject up, and even then he didn't talk about it at length. I asked him what he thought of the documentaries that had been made about Sea Shepherd, and he had the same criticism of all of them: "They focus too much on me." Paul never really wanted to be a hero, but he became one in spite of himself, and I think that he could easily have done without it. That's what makes all the difference, and what makes his commitment truly heroic.

Through spending time with Paul, I learned to love the human being behind the public persona. I cannot say with any degree of certainty whether it is the hero that I met or the friend that he became that has inspired me the most.

Paul is far from being the character described by his opponents. He does not even match up with the self-image that he projects.

However, it does not surprise me that those who have confronted him in the media or at sea (whether they be participants at camps for well-intentioned ecologists or poachers) find him arrogant. What can be perceived as arrogance is rooted in his extraordinary determination and the distance he puts between himself and any criticism or flattery. It is very difficult to upset Paul. In fact, I would say that it is almost impossible. Indeed, he excels at interacting with groups of non-supporters, and such encounters highlight his debating skills.

Paul's irreverence is relevant; he is a forthright rebel. He is not afraid of calling into question the assumptions that pass for absolute truths in our anthropocentric societies. He upsets the status quo, even if it means shocking people and even if it means being the odd man out. "I never set out to win any popularity contests," he has said. "Nothing that I do is done to please people; I work exclusively for the oceans."

Add to that the fact that he makes no concessions for human overpopulation, and he is labeled a misanthropist — which, by the way, does not bother him in the least. In my opinion, Paul is indeed a misanthropist, but one who is especially kind to those who are dear to him and who is fair to all.

He is a complex character and a formidable enemy. But he never crushes or neglects the weakest and most vulnerable. I remember one occasion when he was taking a strip off a well-known artist who had painted a gigantic fresco in support of Sea Shepherd. Many anonymous volunteers had participated in the group project, but the artist had claimed sole credit for the work. In Paul's eyes, the artist lost stature because of his lack of gratitude to the volunteers. Paul doesn't necessarily respect those who are famous or powerful, but he has the utmost respect for those who do not walk all over those who are not.

Shannon Mann, a friend and Sea Shepherd veteran, told me a story that is a good example of how Paul treats the underdog: "I was working late one night at the Friday Harbor office when Paul came in. He said: 'It's very odd, but I just found a little mouse outside. It didn't appear to be injured or anything, it was just sitting there, not moving a muscle. So I picked it up and put it into a shoe box. I hope it is doing okay.' It was a shoe box with all the comforts including food, water and a litter box. Unfortunately, when Paul came back the following day, the mouse was dead. I got the feeling that Paul was saddened by it. He spends his days fighting to defend the largest creatures on the planet, but the little ones also have a place in his heart."

That Paul, and the eco-warrior Paul, provided equal inspiration for my decision to make a commitment to Sea Shepherd. He is one of those people who lift you up and who show you that, among other things, the limits of the possible can be pushed. Paul didn't inspire me to make my commitment to nature, but he certainly provided another dimension for my commitment. I was born and grew up in the Paris suburbs surrounded by pavement, far from the sea, the forest and the mountains. And yet, when I was a little girl, the story of Dian Fossey, who died protecting the gorillas, was really upsetting and for a long time I refused to watch the film that tells the story of her life. When I met Paul for the first time, he asked me if I thought I could risk my own life to save a whale, even though I had never even seen one. But I knew the answer: it didn't matter that I hadn't seen one. And seven years later, after a number of campaigns at sea, after having seen the whales, I know why I didn't need to think about it back then. I had no choice but to make that commitment. Meeting Paul Watson and having the opportunity to spend time with him was a much more powerful motivating force than the master's degree in ecology I received from Pierre-and-Marie-Curie University. University students are not taught to be passionate. But, to be fair, of the fifty or so professors I encountered during the course of my studies, three of them really inspired me; three of them had ecological convictions and knew how to pass them on to their students and make them think beyond the conventions of our anthropocentric and consumer-driven societies. I would like to pay homage to them: Jacques Weber, Gilles Boeuf and Patrick Lavelle. Paul often talks about the three professors as individuals who are making a contribution to changing the world, who are trying to steer it in the right direction. They alone are justification enough for all the time I spent sitting behind a desk at the university, when all I really wanted was to go to sea with Sea Shepherd.

I think I was born at a crucial time. Children today will have nothing left to save once they become adults, if my generation (I am 32 years old) does not take action today to save what is left. Everything will depend on what happens in the next 10 years. And, with the future hanging in the balance, 10 years is a short time. I swing back and forth between hope and despair; I hope that we wake up in time to put the machine into reverse and disprove the dire predictions for the future of the biosphere and humanity.

This book is a compilation of many conversations I had with Paul during our campaigns at sea, in Parisian bistros during his many trips to France, at conferences where I served as his interpreter, and as part of the interviews that I attended or took part in.

In many ways, meeting Paul was one of the most memorable moments in my life. He often says that he cannot think of a better legacy for his time on this earth than having contributed to saving the whales and other marine animals. That's true. But he will have left behind another legacy, which is far from negligible: he will have inspired thousands of people, shaped minds and shaken up the status quo. He is, and in the opinion of many people always will be, a hero. And yet, it is Paul rather than the hero that I like best about Captain Watson.

— Lamya Essemlali
Executive Director of Sea Shepherd France

"I was put on this earth to send the *Sierra* to the bottom. If I accomplish nothing else in my lifetime, ending the career of that one vessel will have sufficed to give it meaning."

— Captain Paul Watson

CHAPTER

1

THE END
OF THE
Sierra

In less than a year, we had wiped out the jewels of the North Atlantic pirate whaler fleet. The Icelandic and Norwegian whalers would be next in line. No one had been hurt, and thousands of whales would live and give birth because we had taken action.

The *Sierra* was a pirate whaler that illegally killed close to 25,000 whales. Its modus operandi involved harpooning every whale that crossed its path regardless of species, gender, age or size. It killed without regard for the season and ignored any hunting laws and regulations. In the interest of saving money, cold harpoons were frequently used to kill the whales. In other words, explosive-tipped harpoons were not used, and this practice prolonged their agony to a considerable degree. The ship had become the prime target of the anti-whaling movement. Everyone agreed that it had to be stopped, but no one had managed to actually do it. The *Sierra* continued to sail the seas all over the world, killing thousands of whales. And the cries of protest from the ecologists were doing nothing to change that fact.

I was getting tired of all the talk and the lack of results. In 1977, I began to work on a plan that would put the *Sierra* out of commission once and for all. At that time, Greenpeace was on the verge of sending the *Ohana Kai* to the scrapheap, so I offered them the symbolic amount of one dollar for it. I told them that I intended to use it to destroy the *Sierra*'s stern ramp, the one used to hoist the whales aboard the vessel. They refused to let me have it; they said my plan was too violent for them. As I didn't have a nickel to my name, I wrote to all the associations I knew of. I got a response from only one of them — a letter from Cleveland Amory, the founder and executive director of the Fund for Animals, based in New York. Even though he thought it was somewhat risky, Cleveland allowed himself to be convinced. He wanted to see the *Sierra* put out of commission as much as I did. He helped me to acquire an old 200-foot British trawler, the *Westella*. It was solid enough for the purpose I had in mind. On December 5, 1978, just three days after my twenty-eighth birthday, I renamed it *Sea Shepherd*: the first ship in history whose sole purpose was to defend marine life.

The first item on the agenda was to locate the *Sierra*. Greenpeace had been investigating it for a number of years and had precious information about its movements. I called John Fritzell, who I had hired to join the Greenpeace team a few years earlier. In the meantime, he had become the Executive Director of the organization. When I asked him if he knew of the *Sierra*'s location, he said: "We might know, but that's classified Greenpeace information. And the *Sea Shepherd* is not part of Greenpeace." I was also in need of a crew. Despite the discouraging start of our conversation, I asked if Greenpeace could spread the word among its volunteers that I was looking for people willing to help out with the mission. "Impossible, we need all of our volunteers to get ready for a fund-raising marathon. The funds raised will be used to buy a vessel to hunt down the whalers." "But I already have a boat," I said. "Couldn't you just ask some of your volunteers if they want to sail with us? A few dedicated souls would suffice." "No, your boat is not a Greenpeace vessel." In the end, I recruited the core crew by placing an ad in the *Boston Globe* and the *Boston Herald American*.

I managed to pinpoint the *Sierra's* approximate location on my own. It was in the Atlantic, somewhere between the Bay of Biscay and the African coast. We were tracking it down, not far from the Portuguese coast, when we crossed paths with some leatherback turtles. I decided to shut off the engines to avoid harming them. We got into the water and swam with them for hours. It was incredible; they were all around us, thousands of them. I had never seen anything like it, nor have I seen anything to compare with it since. Six hours later, we got under way again. The following day, I saw a ship on the horizon. As we got closer to it, we could see that it looked like a whaling ship. Then, the "S" on the hull came into view: it was the *Sierra*. It was headed south and we were headed east. If we had not come across the turtles, we would have missed it. We headed toward them at full speed. They had heard about us, so as soon as they saw us, they made a run for it. We were about 200 miles from the Portuguese coast and they were making for that same coast in order to seek protection from military vessels in the area. Our boat was a little faster than theirs, so we were able to catch up with them without too much difficulty. But the sea had gotten rough and I wanted to make sure that no one got hurt, so we settled for following closely behind them as far as Porto. They had no doubt entered the port to get instructions, and the following day they were ready to leave. I requested permission from the harbormaster to leave port, but was told that we could not leave before the end of the afternoon. It was obvious that they were trying to help the *Sierra* to get away from us.

I called a crew meeting — there were 20 of us on board — and I told them: "I cannot guarantee that you won't get hurt, or worse, but in any case I am going to ram those bastards right here, as they leave port. If you want to leave, now is the time." Ten minutes later, 17 of them were on the wharf with their bags. Peter Woof and Jerry Doran were the only two to remain on board with me. Luckily, they were both mechanics. That was all I really needed. We let go the mooring lines and left port at full speed, closing in on the *Sierra*, which was getting away. I hit it head on in order to get their full attention and also to destroy the harpoon. Then we turned and hit it side on, doing 15 knots. A crack developed in the hull, above the waterline. It then headed back to port, while we headed for England. But a few hours later, a Portuguese destroyer pulled up alongside us and ordered us to follow it to port. Its crew threatened to shoot at us if we did not follow their orders.

Experience has taught me that I should have called their bluff and refused to follow them, but at the time I still had much to learn, as it was my first campaign of that kind. And so, we agreed to follow them. The next day, I appeared before the harbormaster, who wanted to find me guilty of "criminal negligence." I informed him that there was no negligence on our part; we hit the boat in the exact spot where we had intended to hit it. The harbormaster replied: "The problem is that I don't even know who owns the *Sierra* and, without that information I cannot find you guilty of negligence. Therefore you are free to go." The *Sierra* was a phantom ship, and Sea Shepherd could not be sentenced for having rammed a ship that, officially speaking, did not exist. The harbormaster seized my ship nonetheless and so I left for the United States to inform the media of the *Sierra's* misdeeds and the reasons why we had rammed it. A few months later, I went back to Porto to reclaim the *Sea Shepherd*. The *Sierra's* insurer refused to pay the bill for the damage we had inflicted on the hull, the cost of which amounted to one million dollars. The court decided to award the whalers my ship as compensation, unless I could pay the sum of $750,000 ... for a ship that had cost me only $120,000! Some journalists informed me that the judge presiding over the case had received the sum of $60,000 from Andrew Behr, the *Sierra's* owner, who at long last had been identified. I called Peter Woof, who was in Scotland at the time, and I told him that I needed his help to recover *Sea Shepherd*. We entered the port of Porto during the night of December 29, 1979, with the intention of starting up the engines and slipping quietly away. But the boat had been plundered. There wasn't a drop of fuel left, and most of the pumps and the wheelhouse equipment had disappeared. Leaving aboard the boat would obviously be impossible. The idea that the *Sea Shepherd* would be converted into a whaler was one that we could not accept. During the night of December 31, Peter, Lins and I went aboard with a wrench and some flashlights. We went to the engine room and removed the bolts holding the sea water inlet valve in place. A jet of water about 15 feet high shot up violently into the room. The water was already up to our ankles as we left the ship. I left with a heavy heart that night ... *Sea Shepherd's* fate was sealed.

We managed to leave the country by slipping by the military police, even though they had cordoned off the train station and the airport in an attempt to arrest us.

In the meantime, the repairs to the *Sierra* had been completed. In less than a month, the killing would start again.

On the morning of February 6, 1980, I was in a courtroom in Quebec to appear before the judge on charges of interfering with the seal hunt, when an explosive charge placed in the forward section of the whaler sent it to the bottom in the port of Lisbon. The owner had just spent a million dollars to make it seaworthy again, and a few days before it was due to leave port, a fatal blow brought a definitive end to the career of the death ship. I, of course, was suspect No. 1. But it's hard to find a better alibi than being present in a courtroom.

A few weeks later, on April 28, the Spanish whalers *Isba I* and *Isba II* had their turn, when they, too, sank, this time in the port of Vigo. The pirate whaler *Astrid*, which belonged to the same owner as that of the *Sierra*, also went down. Sea Shepherd offered a reward of $25,000 to anyone who could sabotage it, a tempting offer for its own underpaid crew. Two weeks after word of the reward was made public, the owners of the *Astrid* sold it to a Korean fishing company that converted it into a trawler.

In less than a year, we had wiped out the jewels of the North Atlantic pirate whaler fleet. The Icelandic and Norwegian whalers would be next in line. No one had been hurt, and thousands of whales would live and give birth because we had taken action. A few determined souls, a few well-placed mines and good media support had accomplished what a decade of negotiations, compromises and discussions had failed to do. Greenpeace stepped forward to publicly accuse me of being a terrorist. Some thought I was a fanatic, others believed I was a hero. But none of that mattered to me. I left those who refused to act and the moralizers to condemn me and to discuss the matter at length. They will continue to do nothing more, right up until the death of the very last whale.

I had chosen another route.

— Paul Watson
Founder, Sea Shepherd

"They suffer a great deal when the ferocious whalers attack their offspring ... Even though they could dive to safety, they stay on the surface and endanger themselves in order to follow the small floating body."

— Jules Michelet, *La Mer*

CHAPTER

MEETING PAUL WATSON

Children know what is happening, but we make them unlearn it. Then, as they grow up, they become less and less aware of important things such as ecological problems. I can guarantee that a six-year-old child is more aware of what is happening in the world than the average adult. But we quash that passion.

LAMYA ESSEMLALI: After nearly four decades, what is it that keeps you involved despite the obstacles, the problems and the critics? Everyone who began this struggle with you has gone in a different direction; they all ended up moving on to something else. What makes you different?

CAPTAIN PAUL WATSON: I never made a conscious decision to fight the sealers and the whalers. I never felt that I had any choice in the matter. I have seen what men are capable of doing on the ice floes and I have seen what they do on the high seas. I have experienced horror, and it has penetrated the very core of my being. I have seen baby seals being skinned alive, I have been dealt blows by the same ignorant brutes who kill the seals. I have seen whales — magnificent, intelligent creatures — subjected to endless agony. I have heard their cries as they die, drowning in their own blood. I will fight until the bitter end. I will never give up the fight to the barbarians and the bureaucrats. I think that what we are doing is just and in the best interests of our planet and our future. The best job is a job that you can do every day without feeling the need or desire for a vacation and without thoughts of retirement. I have the perfect job and I cannot imagine that I will stop doing it one day. We will make the necessary sacrifices. We will go to prison. We will risk our vessels and our lives. Giving up has never been an option. The idea has never entered my mind.

Do you sometimes get discouraged?

Giving up is not part of my philosophy. I learned from the Lakota — an American Sioux people — that warriors must always focus on the action rather than the result. We do what we do because we cannot imagine not doing it. It is the only right thing to do. I never think about winning or losing. It is a matter of living in the present; the future will be what it must be. What matters is that all of your energy be directed toward achieving your goals, toward what you are doing in the present. What matters, is what you do today.

What do you think of the lack of interest in environmental issues? As a person who is passionate about what is happening to our biodiversity and our planet, it must be frustrating to be faced with indifference.

That doesn't really matter to me. People make a choice to listen or to not listen. It reminds me of the Indian proverb, "Tell people once. If they don't listen, it's not your problem. Continue on anyway."

Who inspires you?

My greatest source of inspiration is a sperm whale. When I looked into the eyes of the dying whale, I saw pity for us, its executioners, who destroy life and display so much ignorance and so little respect and empathy. That day in 1975 changed my life and made me an eco-centric person. In other words, I think that other species are not inferior to humans. On that day, I pledged allegiance to the victims of humanity and I stopped serving the egotistical aspirations of our species. In the conservation field, a number of people have inspired me: Grey Owl for his work with beavers, Dian Fossey, Jane Goodall and Biruté Galdikas for their work with primates, Dr. David Suzuki, the poet and writer Farley Mowat, Robert Hunter, Dr. Carl Sagan, Captains Jacques-Yves Cousteau, Albert Falco and many others. In terms of films and activism in the arts, I have a lot of respect for Jacques Perrin, James Cameron and Martin Sheen, among others. When it comes to poetry, it was Leonard Cohen who gave the desire to write. In terms of strategy, I would name Marshall McLuhan, Sun Tzu, Miyamoto Musashi and James I. Waddell, Captain of the *CSS Shenandoah*. Captain Waddell was hired by the government of the Confederate States of America during the Civil War. His mission involved seeking out and destroying all Union ships in areas where it was not normally possible to do so. He hunted down merchant marine ships headed for the capes of the Southern Ocean and the seal- and whale-hunting areas of North America. Dozens of ships, most of them whaling ships, were sent to the bottom by the *Shenandoah*. That had a huge impact on the whaling industry and enemy business in general. It is not well known, but the Civil War helped save three species of whales by destroying more than 200 whaling ships. Waddell contributed to that, and he did it without killing a single person. His deeds are an example to us because he practiced non-violent aggression. I would also add that my daughter Lilliolani is a great source of inspiration for me.

Speaking of your daughter, some committed activists are often judged in that regard, and have been accused of neglecting their families.

It's important for families to be close, but the family is also a concept that the government uses to control us. Many people tell me that they would like to help me protect at-risk species and habitats, but they say they cannot help out because of family obligations. Family values have become a means of distraction. Concentrating on the nuclear family has led us to neglect and ignore the natural family. We share this planet with millions of other species, but we forget about their interests at our risk and peril. We must put an end to this vicious cycle and the limits within which we live for the sole purpose of perpetuating the family name.

In the end, what is the point of having a family without a healthy environment to make life possible and decent? Conserving and protecting the planet's capacity to sustain life must be a priority for each and every one of us; perhaps that is all the more true for those of us who have a family. I would add that following one's own path is, in my opinion, the most important example a father or mother can give their child.

Have you tried to pass on your passion for protecting nature to your daughter?

I have always told my daughter that she should do as she wishes and choose her own path. I said to her: "Lani, I am not your boss; no one is your boss. You are your only boss. It's your life, you have choices to make; never let a man or anyone else tell you what is best for you. Always listen to your own heart." My daughter is very interested in what I am doing and she has taken part in a number of Sea Shepherd campaigns. But she has chosen her own path, and today she is a talented and accomplished young woman who has made me a very happy father.

Children are, without a doubt, the most passionate of the Sea Shepherd supporters. Often, they seem to be more aware of what is happening at the global level. They also seem to have kept their capacity for wonder and revolt.

When my daughter was a child, she came home from school one day with a note from one of her teachers. He said that he was concerned about her anti-social tendencies. He was concerned because of her answer to the question: "What is your definition of government?" Her answer was: "It is a group of people who join forces to kill other people and animals." Personally, I think that's the right answer!

People often wonder what we should tell our children. In my opinion, we shouldn't tell them anything. I think it is time for us to stop telling and start listening. Children can tell us things without worrying about seeming childish and they are, in fact, often closer to the truth.

So, it is up to us to ask them what they can teach us.

The Sea Shepherd Board of Advisors consists of scientists, lawyers, celebrities and children. One of them is a ten-year-old Australian girl named Isabel Dow. She is one of the most passionate people I have ever known. She organized her own demonstration, at her neighborhood supermarket, to protest the sale of shark meat. Because of her young age, the local press became interested and passed on the story. That's how she managed to get her message out.

Children know what is happening, but we make them unlearn it. Then, as they grow up, they become less and less aware of important things such as ecological problems. I can guarantee that a six-year-old child is more aware of what is happening in the world than the average adult. But we quash that passion. And that's what we lose when we become adults.

You chose to study linguistics. Why didn't you study ecology or marine biology?

Studying communications provides the best possible foundation for developing good strategies and solving all kinds of problems. Language fascinates me, even if the English language is still a challenge for me, as a poet. The activists who are the most influential are not the ones who have studied ecology or marine biology. The key to success is in the arts, music, literature, oral presentations, movies, television, etc. Greenpeace, for example, was founded by a group of journalists. Dr. David Suzuki left the world of science and went into television. Sea Shepherd's success lies in our films, our television series, our writings and public conferences.

"Be sure you're right, then go ahead."

— Davy Crockett

CHAPTER

A PASSIONATE LIFELONG ACTIVIST

Whales are dying, they are being massacred under horrific conditions and so I don't have time to listen to what people have to say. All I know is that thousands of whales are free to swim around in the ocean today because we took action. In my eyes, that's all that matters.

What do you remember about the time you spent as a poet living on a beach in Greece? Would you swap your life as an activist for that kind of cushy existence?

In 1973 and 1974, I spent six months living on a beach in Rhodes, Greece; I wanted to be a poet. It was a total failure. I simply hadn't had enough life experience to be a poet. But, it was still a very pleasant experience. I spent my time swimming in the Mediterranean every day, living on the beach, studying local history, listening to Greek music, drinking retsina and dancing. I enjoyed every minute of it. I have no regrets about the course my life took after that.

You once beat a swimming record. Can you tell me about that?

In 1982, I swam across the Georgia Strait in British Columbia, from Nanaimo on Vancouver Island to Jericho Beach in the city of Vancouver. It took me 27 hours to swim the 35 miles. I planned it so that my departure coincided with the high tide, which brought me out into the Strait; for the arrival, the low tide brought me straight into the city of Vancouver. I was 31 years old at the time and it was the most grueling physical experience that I have ever endured.

You were involved in other ecological struggles in the past, including deforestation and the massacre of wolves and elephants. Why, in the end, did you decide to focus on protecting the oceans?

I have been an activist since I was 11 years old. But I never made a conscious decision to become one; it's something that I grew up with. I got involved in protecting elephants in Kenya, wolves in the Yukon and the forests in British Columbia. I founded organizations like Earthforce, Friends of the Wolf and Coeur du bois. I also did some work with the Sierra Club, Defenders of Wildlife and the Fund for Animals. All of those experiences were beneficial, but it became too much to manage. In order to be more effective, I needed to focus on one specific area. I didn't really choose to defend the oceans; circumstances influenced the path I eventually chose. With my navigation experience, my love of the sea and the fact that I spent my childhood in a fishing village, my exclusive focus on the oceans just came naturally.

You do not campaign against captivity, but you do have strong opinions about it.

The captivity industry finances the massacre of dolphins in Taiji, Japan. The idea that dolphinariums are an educational tool is a heresy. A dolphinarium is a circus where the animals are condemned to die after living out their bleak existence. The time that I spent in prison taught me that incarceration is a form of torture. It gave me a sense of how much animals must suffer when they are in captivity. In my opinion, they would be better off dead. What's more, the emergence of aquariums and dolphinariums in Africa, Asia, South America and Eastern Europe is resulting in increased rates of captures from natural environments!

How does the transition from protester to activist take place? What does it take to be an "eco-warrior"?

There are many ways to contribute to this movement, but the method I chose, namely Sea Shepherd, involves direct opposition to destructive and extremely lucrative activities. And so, it means taking risks with your freedom and your life. When we say that you have to be ready to die in order to become a crew member on one of our ships in order to save whales, it's not rhetoric; it's the reality of the situation. And it's something to keep in mind before getting involved. When I decided to ram the pirate whaler the *Sierra* in 1979, before going ahead with it I gave my crew the choice of staying aboard or going ashore. Only two stayed aboard with me.

After we did it, and came out of it alive and without being sued, one of the people who chose to go ashore said to me: "If I had known you were going to come out of it alive, I would have stayed aboard." But the fact is that we can never be sure that we are going to come out of any intervention unscathed. Going into combat and agreeing to accept any and all consequences is the ultimate test. It is not a question of taking unnecessary risks, but taking action like we do requires the ability to overcome the fear of death. Personally speaking, I never fear for my own life. I don't know why. Perhaps it's denial, or maybe it's a question of understanding the danger and taking it at face value.

I also think it's important to avoid taking action based on the likelihood of a successful outcome. It's a matter of disconnecting your motivation from the probability of victory.

This movement has always taken one step forward and two steps backward, but that's always better than taking three steps backward. I, personally, am convinced that the losing battles are the ones that are worth fighting. With an ever-growing human population, we can only gain extra time for plants, animals and natural habitats. It's a constant battle and I don't know what the outcome will be. But I do know that I must do what I think is right. I have been fighting this battle for 40 years and I will continue to do so until the day I die.

When I first met you, I was very impressed by your ability to resist horror. You are passionate to the point of committing your entire life to this battle and at the same time you have the ability to keep a safe distance, which allows you to avoid becoming completely destroyed, emotionally speaking. I so often hear people say that they love animals so much that they could never put up with the horror, so they are opting for self-preservation. I never wanted to be like that and, when I got to know you, I learned how to construct a kind of mental armor. I think that is surely a non-negotiable criterion for anyone who wants to get involved on the front lines. You cultivate that distance in a number of areas. Aside from your close friends and a few people whom you hold in high esteem, you are relatively indifferent about what people think of you, generally speaking. Flattery and criticism seem to just bounce off you without actually striking you.

One of the things that I have learned over the years is that in order to do what we do, we have to be immune to criticism.

In 1986, we sank half of the Icelandic whaling fleet while the vessels were tied up at the dock. And we destroyed the whale meat–processing plant. That resulted in a loss of $10 million for the whaling industry, from which it took 17 years to recover. At that time, John Fritzell was the executive director of Greenpeace, and he publicly took me to task. He said that what I had done was reprehensible, irresponsible and a disgrace to the ecology movement. To which I replied, "OK, John. But, what does that matter?" He came back with: "I thought that you should know what people in the ecology movement think of you." I shot back, "Quite frankly, John, I don't give a damn. We didn't sink those whaling ships for you, your Greenpeace or anybody else. We sank them for the whales." Whales are dying, they are being massacred under horrific conditions and so I don't have time to listen to what people have to say. All I know is that thousands of whales are free to swim around in the ocean today because we took action. In my eyes, that's all that matters. That, and the fact that we intervened without injuring anyone. Then I added, "John, if you can find one whale who disapproves of what we did in Iceland, I might reconsider." Whales, dolphins, sharks and all the other creatures that live in the sea are our clients. We represent them and we work for them.

Lots of people would like to be able to free themselves of the opinions of other people. But it requires real strength of character to completely disconnect your actions from the judgments they may trigger. How do you do it?

I had a life-changing experience that helped me to immunize myself against criticism from my peers. I was with Greenpeace at the time, and we had located the Soviet whaling fleet about 60 nautical miles from Eureka, California. At that time, our approach to saving whales involved forming human shields by positioning ourselves in front of the explosive-tipped harpoons; I was reading a lot of Gandhi at the time. Bob Hunter (one of the Greenpeace co-founders) and I were in a little boat. Behind us was a 150-foot Soviet harpoon vessel. In front of us, eight magnificent sperm whales were making a break for it. Each time the whalers tried to shoot, we would maneuver the boat into position in their line of fire. The strategy was working until the captain of the whaler came out and shouted something into the harpooner's ear. He looked at us, drew his finger across his throat from ear to ear and smiled. I then understood that Gandhi's method was not going to work for us.

A few seconds later, an incredible explosion ripped through the air. The harpoon flew over our heads and planted itself in the back of a female sperm whale. She screamed out in a woman-like voice, then rolled over in a fountain of blood. At the same time, the largest whale in the group, a male, beat the surface with his tail, then disappeared. He went underneath our little boat and came up into the air in attack mode, right in front of the harpoon. But they were ready for him. They shot him in the head, at close range. The sperm whale went into violent contortions and I caught his eye for a brief moment. Suddenly, he dove again; all I could see from the surface was a line of bloody bubbles, heading straight for us. He surfaced again right over our boat and straightened out. The entire length of his body was towering over us, so that all he had to do was let himself fall on us and we would have been swallowed up by the sea. But our eyes met again, his eye was right above my head; it was the size of my fist. What I saw in the eye of the sperm whale that day changed my life forever. He could have killed us; if he had just let himself fall toward us he would have crushed us. But, in his eyes I saw understanding. He understood what we were trying to do. His muscles contracted, and with enormous effort, he began to back away. As he fell slowly into the water, I saw his eye disappear under the surface. That's how he died.

He could have killed us, but he chose not to do it. Since that time, I have felt that I owe him an enormous debt, and that is one of the reasons why I have devoted my life to whales.

Something struck me that day, something else that I had seen in the sperm whale's eye. Aside from the comprehension of what was happening, I also saw pity in his eye. Pity for us humans, who are able to kill without mercy. I started thinking about it: why were the Russians killing these whales? They were hunting the sperm whales to obtain spermaceti, a lubricating oil that can withstand very high temperatures. Spermaceti is used to manufacture intercontinental ballistic missiles, among other things. We were killing these magnificent, extremely intelligent and socially complex creatures in order to manufacture weapons of mass destruction so that we can kill each other. That's when I really understood that humans are crazy.

Something in me changed on that day; from that time forward, I stopped doing things for people and started working exclusively for whales and other marine creatures.

"It is sad to think that nature is talking and the human race is not listening."

— Victor Hugo

CHAPTER

4

HUMAN VERSUS
NATURE

The fact is that we are going to lose more species of plants and animals between 2000 and 2065 than the planet has lost over the past 65 million years. We are at the height of a mass extinction crisis. This age of extinction is called the Anthropocene because Homo sapiens *are responsible for it.*

Ecologists and those who defend animals are often criticized for not placing the priority on human beings. This opposition between the interests of nature and the interests of humanity is a major obstacle to progress in the conservation movement.

Out of every dollar that I donate to charitable works, 99 cents is used to solve human problems or support human causes. The remaining cent is used to defend the planet and all other species. Some people would like us to donate even more to defend people and less to defend the planet. And while we cannot eliminate cancer, we can wipe out the main causes. We are the ones who have allowed the disease to reach the magnitude it has reached; it is the consequence of what we inflict on the planet and on ourselves. And so, we spend almost all of our available charitable resources to combat poverty, AIDS, cancer and all sorts of problems that were to a large extent created by human beings, while the solutions can be found in nature. We spend these funds in the worst possible ways, by lining the pockets of greedy people. The irony of all this is that defending ecosystems is more important than anything else. If the oceans die, we will all die. Therefore, saving the fish, the sea birds and the plankton is more important than finding a cure for cancer. This type of position makes me politically incorrect, but that matters very little to me. I would prefer, by far, to be ecologically correct.

What are the essential differences between the human rights movement and the conservation movement?

The human rights and nature conservation movements come into conflict with each other when human rights are used to justify the massacre of a vulnerable species or the destruction of a natural habitat in the name of culture, race or tradition. I think that the survival rights of one species should prevail over the right of any human or group of humans to kill or destroy it. The first cause of mass extinction is the destruction of natural habitats due to the human population explosion. Merely discussing these questions leads to accusations of racism and misanthropy.

There are no political trends with respect to conservation. All conservationists are conservative in the strictest sense of the term. Our goal is to conserve the ecological status quo. Right-wing and left-wing politicians embrace philosophies that are destructive for the environment and short-term goals designed to garner votes.

The human rights movement is, on the other hand, very politicized. Human rights have no meaning if governments can snap their fingers and wipe them out (as was the case with the parodic *Patriot Act*[1] voted in by the government of the United States), or label anyone of their choosing as a "terrorist" without any proof, much like China did when it listed the Dalai Lama as an "official" terrorist, or like Japan, when it listed me as an official "ecoterrorist."

What, in your opinion, is the relationship between environmental and social problems?

I think that social problems are secondary to environmental ones. I think that our priority lies in solving ecological problems. Each decision we make must take into account the interests and needs of other species; we can no longer embrace the anthropocentric thinking that dictates that our interests are the only ones that count. Human beings think they are the only ones that are important, but we must include all other species on the planet if we want to avoid backing into a corner.

We give minimal thought to the role played by plants, insects and fish, the species that make this planet livable for all the other ones, including ourselves. We cannot continue to ignore them and hope to survive. Therefore, in my opinion, non-human rights are as important, if not more important, than human rights.

That kind of statement is the very reason some people call you a misanthropist.

That's very true; I am not a fan of the human species, overall. Of course, I do like some people, but I like them as individuals.

Our behavior toward the planet is comparable to that of a gang of arrogant and completely unruly primates. We behave in an egotistical, greedy and destructive manner with each other and even more so toward other species. We constantly violate the three basic laws of ecology, even though no other species has ever survived on this planet without respecting the basic laws of nature. The world is full of ecological imbeciles who live in denial of the reality of nature. The world is teeming with mindless hordes who live in a fantasy based on religion or entertainment. The world needs ecological engineers and eco-warriors with the will to eliminate the threats that weigh heavily on our planet, and on the oceans in particular.

Ecologically speaking, we are without a doubt the most stupid of all the species. One day, I was arguing with a Norwegian whaler who said to me, "Watson, how can you say that whales are more intelligent than people?!" I replied, "Well, I measure the intelligence of a species based on its ability to live in harmony with the natural world, and according to that criterion, whales are more intelligent than humans." To which he replied, "But if that is the criterion, beetles are more intelligent than we are." So, I said to him, "George, you're beginning to understand what I'm trying to tell you. The big concern is that ecology is a matter of survival, and so we cannot maintain the same level of stupidity much longer."

If humans are the source of the problem, aren't they also the source of the solution?

All human beings need to do is to respect the laws of nature before it's too late. The biggest threat to the planet's biodiversity is the rampant growth of the human population. The more of us there are, the more we will pick away at natural habitats and the planet's ability to sustain us. We are the cause of the massive and current extinction of plants and the reality that we cannot escape is that, without water, we will not survive on this planet.

Ecology is closely tied to economic and social issues, which makes it impossible to exclude the human factor from the general picture. It is often the case that people who poach (not those who purchase their harvest) are poor and subjected to exploitation. The fact that they have to feed their families is the argument most often put forth in support of their activities. That argument is offered up as justification for using dynamite as a fishing method, destroying corals, trafficking bush meat and ivory, etc. These activities are often carried out by desperate people.

Bank robberies, armed robbery, kidnapping, drug trafficking, etc.; it is often the case that desperate people commit these crimes.

Overfishing, poaching, using dynamite and cyanide for fishing, fishing for shark fins, and all other practices that harm the natural equilibrium that people justify by using poverty as an excuse — these are crimes against the planet, crimes against humanity and against the future. Poverty will never be eliminated as long as the growth of human populations continues, as dictated by one basic law of ecology: the law of finite resources. There simply are not enough fish in the sea for an ever-expanding human population. When we eradicate the fish, hundreds of millions of people will die of hunger because there will be nothing left.

Today, 80% of the natural resources are consumed by 20%[2] of the population, and the gap between rich and poor is growing. But we are still hearing that ecological problems are problems for the rich and that the poor have other priorities.

Ecology is everyone's problem. The poor are the first to suffer from ecological problems and they are the ones that suffer the most as a result of them. But the ecological bill will be paid by each human being on this planet. The ever-increasing exploitation of finite resources by the human population is at the heart of the problem. In the end, the poor are people who aspire to becoming rich. The rich rely on an ever-growing population to build a larger and larger consumer base. Because of their massive numbers, the contribution of the poor is equal to that of rich people when it comes to devouring the biosphere. If the rich were to be removed from the equation, the number of poor people would still continue to grow and contribute to impoverishing the planet. If the poor were to be removed, the rich could no longer exploit those resources efficiently, nor could they profit by selling them to the poor.

When there is opposition to an ecologically harmful project, the jobs that are at stake are often used as an argument to justify continuing on with the project. This is the case with the fishing and forestry industries, among others.

I don't see why we should protect people whose work consists of destroying the planet. We do not do that for any other industry. For example, when the spotted owl needed protection, which involved stopping the destruction of forests in the United States, the media harped on about the loss of jobs in the forestry industry. Everyone seemed to be very concerned about that.

While the situation was playing out involving the jobs that were being sacrificed for the sake of the spotted owl, McDonald's, AT&T,

IBM and a few others were laying off 250,000 people in order to satisfy their shareholders. And, oddly enough, the media had hardly a word to say about that. Apparently, that is understandable. But sacrificing 25,000 jobs for an owl? A bird that has evolved over hundreds of millions of years is to be annihilated overnight? Our society does not understand that and does not accept it.

A few years ago, a ranger in Zimbabwe killed a poacher and was harshly criticized by human rights organizations. They reproached him with: "How can you dare take a human life in order to protect an animal?" His reply underscores the hypocrisy of our values: "You know, I don't understand why everyone is so shocked. If I were a police officer in Harare and a man had just robbed Barclay's Bank and was escaping with a bag of money under his arm, and if I were to shoot that man in the head and kill him in the middle of the main street in view of everyone, I would be given a medal and people would call me a hero. How is it possible that a bag full of pieces of paper is more valuable than the future heritage of the country of Zimbabwe?" How is it possible indeed? That is a question to which there really is no answer because we place a higher value on those pieces of paper than we do on a living being.

Are you saying that we are all hypocrites?

The poet Leonard Cohen wrote that "You are locked into your suffering and your pleasures are the seal." We are so preoccupied with seeking out pleasure, with entertaining ourselves, that we aren't doing anything to solve the problems. The Romans understood it perfectly: "Give the people bread and circus games." And that's what we are being given today, bread and circus games. Everything, from drugs to alcohol to TV series, is there for the purpose of brainwashing people and to sell them even more shit. Currently, the number of *Warcraft* video game subscribers is greater than the number of members of all the ecological associations all over the world.

So yes, we are all hypocrites. Everyone is an ecologist until it means giving up something that is essentially superfluous; then, after that point, there are none left.

Too many human beings consume too many resources and violate the basic laws of nature (finite resources, diversity and the interdependence of species). In fact, any human law that breaks these natural laws must be called into question. We will have to rethink them if we want to survive. The fact is that we are going to lose more species of plants and animals between 2000 and 2065 than the planet has lost over the past 65 million years. We are at the height of a mass extinction crisis,[3] and it has a name: the Anthropocene. This age of extinction is called the Anthropocene because *Homo sapiens* are responsible for it.

In 2010, China became the country with the highest level of energy consumption on the planet, a position previously held by the United States. Twenty years ago, China was a poor country. There is no such thing as the rich and the poor. There are the rich, and there are those who aspire to becoming rich. Nobody wants to be poor. The only way to turn things around is to reduce resource consumption rather than increase it. So we need some countries to lower their standard of living, instead of having developing countries increase theirs. But that won't happen, because human beings are profoundly egotistical. We want the maximum for ourselves. People justify the destruction of the oceans by saying that they need to feed their families. They justify the destruction of the forests by arguing that they need to buy a new television, etc. Everyone has a justification, and it is precisely this justification that will be the end of us.

Over the course of this century, we are going to experience ecological collapse. That will happen in the next one hundred years. Everyone who says: "Oh! Ecologists are just being Cassandra-type alarmists" are forgetting one thing. Cassandra was an alarmist, but she was right. If King Priam had listened to his daughter, he could have changed the course of history and saved the city of Troy. That's exactly what is happening today. If we would just listen to the people who are making alarmist predictions, we could change the course of things and save what the future still could be.

But it is not very likely that that will happen because human beings have an incredible ability to adapt when they are subjected to extreme pressure. And so, it is really only when things are on the verge of collapsing that we will finally say: "Oh, okay. Maybe we will have to manage this situation ... " The people who understand what is happening must prepare themselves and their children, because the world that they were born into is going to change dramatically. We have a choice between committing mass suicide and waking up and fighting for our survival.

In any case, the one sure thing is that we do not have much time.

"We do not inherit the Earth from our ancestors,
we borrow it from our children."
                    — Native American Proverb

CHAPTER

HUMANS IN *H*ARMONY WITH NATURE

We have to understand that it's a question of making a real commitment; our ultimate goal is to ensure that the continuum of life on this planet can be maintained. Most people do not think about the future very much because we are trapped in the media culture that is defining our own reality.

You ou were involved in activism alongside American Indians in the 1970s. Doesn't that mean that you have some interest in the fate of humans who are treated unjustly?

Indigenous cultures tend to be biocentric and so I think of them as allies. The Lakota fought to save the bison, and that's why I volunteered to support them at Wounded Knee in 1973. It's also the reason why I joined forces with the Mohawk and why our ships fly the flag of the Iroquois Five Nations. I supported the Kayapos Indians in Brazil because they were opposing the construction of a dam on the Xingu River, and I have also supported the Australian Aboriginals. All of those indigenous peoples have one thing in common: they place the earth and other species before themselves.

I often ask people the following question: "What is the name of your great-great-great-grandmother who was alive around the year 1550?" No one knows and no one cares. Why? Because it's not part of our reality. I found an Australian Aboriginal who was able to give me an answer. Not only did he know her name, he was also able to tell me about some of the details of her life.

Aboriginal peoples around the world know where they come from, and so they know who they are and where they are going. That's a lesson that they could teach us. Because their roots matter to them, their future also matters. And so any children who are born, even in the very distant future, are an integral part of their present reality. They will never see the flesh-and-blood child, but knowledge that the child will exist is enough for them to feel concern and to conduct themselves accordingly. And that's the very thing that should motivate all of us: tomorrow will not be possible unless we take action today.

Being an ecologist means being a part of the continuum of life. It's not about being concerned about what the world will be like in 10 years, or even one hundred years. Everything we do today will have a significant impact on the kind of world that we will leave behind us in one hundred thousand years or one million years. Every species that becomes extinct today because of us will have a ripple effect into the future that will create an incredibly negative impact.

We have to understand that it's a question of making a real commitment; our ultimate goal is to ensure that the continuum of life on this planet can be maintained. Most people do not think about the future very much. We don't pay attention to it, largely because we are trapped in the media culture that is defining our own reality. I have a great deal of respect for Aboriginal cultures because they have the ability to think beyond their own individuality.

Aboriginals put the earth and other species before themselves. Isn't that one of the principles of deep ecology? Do you identify with that philosophy?

Deep ecology puts life at the center of all things, not just human life, but all of life. So, yes, I'm a part of that movement because I support the idea that the biosphere is more important than people. What I mean is, protecting nature protects humanity. That is not an anti-human position; it is simply a realistic approach to the world in which we live, and it would be best if we could all become a little more realistic in the near future, because time is of the essence.

If we want to survive on this planet, we are going to have to understand that we need to respect the laws of ecology:

Law No. 1: The strength of any ecosystem is based on biodiversity. The decreased level of biodiversity on the planet today is our most serious problem, even more serious than global warming.

Because ...

Law No. 2 is interdependence: all species are interdependent; they need each other.

Law No. 3 is the law of finite resources: growth has a limit and there is a limit to the earth's carrying capacity.

We are stealing carrying capacity from other species, which are dying out as our population increases. We can continue on like this only up to a certain point. If the fish disappear, the oceans will die. And if the oceans die, we will die. We cannot live on this planet if the oceans die.

If we think of our planet as a spaceship, it's easier to understand. The earth is currently traveling through the galaxy at high speed. And, like any spaceship, it has a life support system: the biosphere. It provides us with the air that we breathe, the food that we eat and it looks after and manages our waste. In order for the system to remain operational, the spaceship needs a crew. The entire crew is very important; it includes species that we take for granted — bacteria, insects, worms and fish. They make the planet functional. We are the passengers. Some species give, but we only take. We take good times, we have fun and create the various fantasy worlds that we live in. We spend our time killing each other for stupid reasons and we remain completely alienated from the world in which we live. What we need to understand is that we must protect the crew at all costs. If the bees disappear, we will have big problems. If some bacteria disappear, we will die. Humans think that they are independent individual entities that are separate from nature, whereas in reality, each one of us is a symbiotic being.

There are living entities inside of us that keep us alive. As we speak, close to 800 species of bacteria are decomposing our food, making it possible to absorb the vitamins and keep us alive. Our body consists of 1,012 cells, on average, and we live in symbiosis with 1,214 microorganisms. Therefore, there are one hundred times more bacteria than cells in our bodies. It is hard to imagine a more intimate connection with nature.

And, as the captain of my ship, if I were to see my mechanics taking rivets out of the walls in the machine room, I would ask them, "What do you think you are doing?" And, if they were to reply, "We can get one dollar for each of these rivets once we get back to Earth." I would say, "Great, I'm in!" only if I were an irresponsible captain. And that is precisely what the presidents and prime ministers are doing today. But if they take out one too many rivets, the wall will come down and the spaceship will not make it back to Earth. If we think of each species as a rivet in the wall of the biosphere, removing one too many will make the whole system fall apart. It would be better for us to avoid testing that hypothesis.

Therefore, if we want to continue behaving as if we could afford to ignore the crew, we will have to face the consequences. I know who my enemy is. It is me and it is each one of us. It is the human species, this hyper-glorified naked primate who, in its own mind, is a divine legend, and who is too stupid and busy entertaining itself to understand that it is on a path that leads straight to evolutionary suicide.

People think that "saving the planet" is the focus of ecology, but the planet has been around much longer than we have, and it will be around long after we are no longer here. But, in reality, it is not a question of preventing the destruction of the planet; it is a matter of transforming it.

What people do not realize is that if we lose the animals, we will all die; the destruction of biodiversity will signal the death of humanity.

That is why the ultimate act of goodwill toward people is to preserve the biosphere that keeps us alive.

For the first time in the history of this planet, one single species is responsible for a mass extinction crisis. The last time that happened, an asteroid crashed into the planet resulting in the extinction of the dinosaurs. It takes between 15 and 20 million years for the earth to recover from a mass extinction crisis, and only if the planet has time, not us. Therefore, it is really a question of saving ourselves; are we intelligent enough to do it, or not? The situation reminds me of the *Titanic*; we are bringing all of the other species down with us. All of the species are going to die out because of our ecological stupidity.

The future that awaits us will include the deterioration of that situation, and ever-increasing pressure will be placed on the ecological community. That will happen and people will suffer. The world that I was born into was populated by some 3 billion people; that population has now reached 7 billion and in 50 years there will be some 12 billion people living on this planet, even if population stabilization in developing countries is visible on the horizon.

Those figures, combined with our consumer lifestyle and hyper-productivity, will necessarily result in ecological collapse in the coming century. Is that the kind of world we want to pass on to our children? Because I can assure you that — even though we don't like to think about it very much and even though we hardly bother to even imagine it — compared with a world in ecological collapse, all the wars, famines and epidemics that have marked the history of the planet will look like a picnic. In a world where 90% of the population dies before the age of 12 months and in which the survivors are reduced to fighting over a few potatoes, we will see how quickly we will fall back into barbarianism. Everything that our human civilizations have accomplished, everything that we have built, all the stories we have told and the songs and poems that we have written will be lost and forgotten. All of that, simply because we did not have the ability to project into the future and forecast the consequences of our actions.

"What the sealers want, is the right to go out there and kill seals. They are entitled to do it, and the more of them they kill, the happier I will be."

— John Efford,
former Minister of Fisheries,
Newfoundland and Labrador

CHAPTER

6

PAUL AND THE ABY SEALS

When Brigitte Bardot came to Newfoundland in 1977 to protest the seal massacre, it created such media hype around the problem that the massacres were prohibited for 10 years. That photo of Brigitte Bardot holding a baby sea in her arms was seen all over the world and saved the lives of millions of seals.

Your friendship with Brigitte Bardot dates back to the 1970s when you invited her to come to the Canadian Grand Banks to protest the famous baby seal massacre. You recently renamed one of your vessels the *Brigitte Bardot*. Sea Shepherd has been criticized for that alliance and for supporting the Brigitte Bardot Foundation because of the star's political views; she is often accused of being a racist.

Brigitte Bardot is a compassionate woman who is concerned about animals and the environment. I don't care one bit about her political views. I have no interest in the different political parties, be they right-wing, left-wing or moderate. The more the human population grows, the more conflicts will emerge between different cultures. Personally, I couldn't care less about human cultures, religions, customs or attitudes, but those who do care about such things might see them as sources of conflict.

The Japanese whalers refer to me as a racist because I oppose their illegal whale hunting and because I despise their strategy, which consists of playing the racist card, even though Japan is one of the most racist societies in the world. One need only ask the Chinese and the Koreans. Japan is one of the only countries in the world that authorizes signs that indicate that non-Japanese are not welcome in some bars and restaurants. I am opposed to massacring whales, dolphins and seals. I am also opposed to illegal fishing, and in order to protest that practice, I have confronted the Japanese, the Soviets, the Norwegians, the Faroe Islanders, the Maltese, the Spanish, the Cubans, the Canadians, the Americans, the Australians, the Ecuadorians, the Costa Ricans, the Taiwanese, the Icelanders, the English, the Irish, the South Africans, the French, the Mexicans, the Namibians, the Italians, the Tunisians and even the Makahs, a Native American tribe.

I don't really want to know about the ethnic origins, culture, nationality, or gender of whoever is destroying marine life; I am opposed to harpoons, clubs, long lines, nets, firearms and longliners. I do not discriminate in my opposition to the people behind those engines of death.

When Brigitte Bardot came to Newfoundland in 1977 to protest the seal massacre, it created such media hype around the problem that the massacres were prohibited for 10 years. The photo of Brigitte Bardot on the Grand Banks holding a baby seal in her arms was seen all over the world. That photo saved the lives of millions of seals and

I have a lot of respect for her because she has been loyal to the animal cause for decades.

Your fight to end the Canadian seal hunt goes back to 1974. Today, the United States, Europe and Russia have banned the importation of seal-based products, which has wiped out the market for them. That marks the end of decades of fighting to end what used to be the biggest massacre of marine mammals in the world.

I was 10 years old when I saw a seal being clubbed to death for the first time on the shore of the Gulf of St. Lawrence, where I grew up. Since that time, it has been my dream to put an end to the seal hunt. And seeing it become a reality has been a long journey; it took close to four decades.

During that time, I brought ships to the seal hunt on six separate occasions: in 1979, 1981, 1983, 1998, 2005 and 2008. I also led three helicopter missions: one in 1976, one in 1977 and one in 1995. During the course of those years, we pushed back sealing ships on the Grand Banks, blocked sealing vessels in ports, walked many miles over hazardous ice fields, confronted Canadian fisheries officers and Royal Canadian Mounted Police officers, debated with senators, parliamentarians, several fisheries ministers and a number of prime ministers. We invited celebrities including Brigitte Bardot, Richard Dean Anderson and Martin Sheen to the Grand Banks and worked to have seal-based products banned throughout the world. We were arrested, struck by the police and the sealers, lost a ship, were defamed throughout Canada and called ecoterrorists, extremists and national traitors.

Sea Shepherd lost a vessel in 2008. The *Farley Mowat* was confiscated and auctioned off by the Canadian government, which accused the organization of violating the *Seal Protection Act*, that prohibited filming or taking photos of the hunt. The Canadian government always claimed that the Newfoundland seal hunt was one of the most humane in the world.

They always tried to mitigate the cruelty of the massacre simply by claiming that it was carried out under "humane" conditions, while prohibiting any independent observation of it, unless the observers were approved by the government. Veterinarians, who were not paid by the government, reported that close to half of the seals were skinned alive. I've seen with my own eyes the way sealers behave with baby seals who are unable to escape from them. I saw them kick them in the head and I saw them gut them while they were still fighting for their lives.

The government employed so-called scientists to tell them what they wanted to hear; I call them "science whores." They are the same people who said that the cod stocks in the northeastern Atlantic were in perfect health up until the day when the collapse occurred, in 1992. They have not yet recovered. The Canadian Department of Fisheries and Oceans has no idea about what it is in the process of doing. There is a long history of mismanagement and incompetence. I came up with a non-lethal alternative, one that is no doubt painless for the seals, which involves brushing them during the molting period to recover their down. I had even found a market in Germany. But Canada refused to give me a license, and the sealers said that they weren't interested in brushing seals; not masculine enough, according to them.

These guys want only one thing; they want to club the seals and skin them. That's what they enjoy doing. Each time we suggested an alternative, it was rejected by the government.

That massacre was an immoral one and it made no ecological or economic sense, and yet it persisted for decades.

The main reason for that is that northeastern Canadians (and I am one of them) are a gang of barbarians, and I mean that in the literal sense. Anyone who meets the inhabitants of the Magdelen Islands and Newfoundland can attest to the fact. They are barbarians in the strictest sense of the term. Michael Dwyer, a seal hunter from the area, wrote a book called *Over the Side, Mickey: A Sealer's First Hand Account of the Newfoundland Seal Hunt.* In it, he says: "The animal rights activists say that we are barbarians, well, you know what? They are right. You have to be a barbarian to do what we do out there." In fact, I recommend his books because he was a fisher and a seal hunter, and if we said even one of the things that he says in his book, no one would have believed us. What he describes is much worse than anything that we saw and documented. Just like the sealer from the Magdelen Islands who said to me one day, "It has nothing to do with money. It's a question of getting away from the wife, going off with your buddies, loading up the cases of beer and killing stuff, see, that's all it is." They enjoy doing it. Just like the Faroe Islanders like killing pilot whales. It is a type of sociopathic behavior that makes people go to war with nature and other species. Why do they do it? Why do serial killers kill people? We don't know, but I think that wild game hunters are emotional and sexual deviants. I think that anyone who feels the need to kill a magnificent animal in order to have its head mounted and hung on the wall suffers from a serious sexual and psychological disorder.

"Every revolution evaporates and leaves behind only the slime of a new bureaucracy."

— Franz Kafka

CHAPTER

7

GREENPEACE,
MY
LOVE

As I said, I mistrust very large organizations. They tend to become corporations or bureaucracies. For the most part, they become good-conscience peddlers and do not do much of anything concrete. In the 1970s, Greenpeace did a lot more with a very small budget than it does today with an annual budget of $300 million.

You often say that the strength of any ecosystem is rooted in biodiversity and that the strength of the ecology movement is anchored in a diversity of approaches and methods; different abilities and qualities provide the most complete strategy possible.

Absolutely. A variety of approaches makes for a strong ecology movement. Unfortunately, a new kind of business has recently emerged. The good-conscience business. People join these organizations in order to feel good about themselves. The organizations hold the reins for you. They say, "We will solve this problem; just send us $30, or $130. Just do that, and we'll look after the problem for you." Greenpeace is one of the only organizations that I would criticize in that regard, because I think of myself as a kind of Dr. Frankenstein. I helped to create a green monster that exists for the sole purpose of perpetuating itself.

A few years ago, Greenpeace spent $49 million to send out 37 million appeals for donations. How can a so-called environmental organization spend such enormous sums of money for the purpose of ... raising even more money?

They know what they are doing; it's all just business. Today, the people who run Greenpeace and similar large organizations are businesspeople, financiers and fund raisers. They do not want to be seen as activists; activists are just a nuisance.

David Brower found that out the hard way when he founded the Sierra Club; he was no longer a welcome member of his own organization when he wanted to take concrete action. He then founded Friends of the Earth, but was eventually forced to leave that organization as well. This happens because, as they get bigger, organizations become too conservative for their founders, and it happens almost systematically.

In my opinion, organizations cannot provide a complete solution, nor can governments. Margaret Mead, a member of the Sea Shepherd Board of Advisors from the very beginning, said that the commitment and actions of individuals has been the only thing that has brought about any significant change over the course of the years.

Would you go as far as to say that big NGOs do more harm than good? Isn't it true that big organizations are useful because they carry more weight at the political level and with the media; aren't they important when it comes to lobbying?

Yes, of course. Strength equals diversity and complementarity, and that exists within large organizations that do positive things. I see these big groups as individuals, and I see that some do positive things while others do not. Small and large organizations both have a role to play, but the biggest structures are more inclined to be influenced by political and economic considerations.

Opinions about Sea Shepherd are far from unanimous, even within the ecology movement. Some organizations approve of our methods, such as WWF France. The former head of its "sustainable fishing" program, Charles Braine, says that your actions are media events that serve as a punch in the face that help to get people talking about these topics and that that is a part of the complementarity of associations. But others are quite critical of them, Greenpeace being the most vocal of those critics. According to that organization, "Sea Shepherd does more harm than good for the environmental cause because the anti-ecologists use the fact that an extreme minority within the ecology movement uses force and sabotage in order to label the entire movement as a terrorist movement. In addition to being a moral error, the use of violence is a tactical error." How do you respond to that?

Sea Shepherd is not a terrorist organization. We have never been found guilty of a single crime (unlike Greenpeace), have never had any serious injuries or deaths (unlike Greenpeace) and we have put an end to many whale-hunting, seal-hunting and illegal fishing operations (unlike Greenpeace). Sea Shepherd does not break the law; we respect the law. Greenpeace has been found guilty of a number of criminal offenses, while Sea Shepherd has not been found guilty of even one.

Other environmental organizations are opposed to us, basically because we do not accept their idea of what we should be. When we go beyond the limit of petitions, lobbying, demonstrations and hanging up banners, we fall into disgrace in the eyes of a large percentage of the "greens." But our goal is not to protest against whale hunting; our goal is to put an end to it. Nor do we exist to serve the ecology movement; we serve the global ecosystem, the marine ecosystem in particular. Sea Shepherd does not adhere to the prejudices and closed-mindedness of these so-called ecology movements. We do not have a right-wing or a left-wing political agenda. We are not part of any specific political trend and we may be politically incorrect, but we try to be ecologically correct.

You are one of the co-founders of Greenpeace (today, Greenpeace denies it). You left that organization in 1979. What do you think of what it has become?

As I said, I mistrust very large organizations. They tend to become corporations or bureaucracies. For the most part, they become good-conscience peddlers that do not do much of anything concrete. In the 1970s, Greenpeace did a lot more with a very small budget than it does today with an annual budget of $300 million.

The thing is, that in order to obtain such a huge amount of funding, they sacrificed the imagination, passion and courage of the people who were really sticking their necks out. All of those people were fired or forced out the door. Not one single original "greenpeacer" is left in today's Greenpeace; they have all been excluded. It is no longer the Greenpeace that I got involved with. Today it is a multinational corporation that calls itself Greenpeace.

The following statement appears on the Greenpeace website: "We think that throwing butyric acid at whaling ships, entangling their propellers with rope and threatening to ram them in the icy waters of the Antarctic constitutes violence because of the potential consequences." By making such statements, Greenpeace is acting as a public relations firm for the whalers and is relaying their anti-Sea Shepherd propaganda. But, they are aware that the "butyric acid" they mention is nothing more than rancid butter, an organic, non-toxic and biodegradable substance that is less acidic than citric acid, also known as orange juice. They also know that the Japanese whaling ships willingly rammed and sunk a Sea Shepherd vessel with six men on board, in the icy waters of the Antarctic that they mention. While virulent in its condemnation of Sea Shepherd, Greenpeace has never condemned the violence perpetrated by the Japanese whalers against our crews.

I was doing a television show in Vancouver when someone called in a bomb scare to protest the violence of my actions, which is quite an incongruous gesture. We had to evacuate the premises. Then, a journalist stuck a microphone in my face and said, "Greenpeace says that you are an ecoterrorist. How do you respond to that?" I replied, "What else can we expect from the Tupperware ladies of the ecology movement?" They never forgave me for that remark. But they had called me an ecoterrorist and I was simply reacting to that.

A few years ago, the Australian show *60 Minutes* aired an episode in which one of the Greenpeace spokespeople says that they are opposed to Sea Shepherd because of the violence involved in our activities, while the Greenpeace approach consists of simply bearing witness. I was floored. To be content with bearing witness ...! If you were walking down the street and saw a woman being assaulted, you would not be content with merely bearing witness. If you saw a puppy or a kitten being tortured, you would not be content with being a mere witness. If you saw a child being ill-treated, you would not be satisfied with taking a photo. And you don't go to Antarctica, a place where you can see the whales dying, in order to fly banners and take photos, or to simply bear witness. In my opinion, the strategy of bearing witness is just another form of laziness. I was very, very shocked to hear that.

Our organization prefers taking action to protesting. Protesting belies an underlying attitude of submission; it amounts to begging: "Please, please don't kill the whales!" Knowing that they will be killing them in any case — they don't care at all about any pleas. Killing whales is illegal and the protest phase is over. Now it's time to put an end to it. But we must do it responsibly; in other words, without harming anyone.

But, can't we think of the different approaches as serving different purposes? Can an organization like Greenpeace, which focuses on communications and lobbying, be seen as being complementary to Sea Shepherd?

The strength of any organization is indeed rooted in diversity, but that is not the kind of diversity I was thinking of. A variety of approaches must be found in legislation, education, direct action, etc. What's more, there is a fault-line in the movement, namely the part motivated by profit, which exists for the sole purpose of perpetuating itself, and most large organizations fall into that category. Dian Fossey is a good example of this. She was a woman of boundless passion who worked to protect mountain gorillas. She would have to beg large organizations for every cent to fund her work. She would be given five or ten thousand dollars. Meanwhile, those same organizations mounted massive campaigns based on her activities and they would collect millions of dollars because of what she was doing. The money would flood in, but, unfortunately for her, the funding problems persisted. And when she started to become entrenched in her position toward the poachers, and to put forth suggestions for ways to stop them, the organizations would threaten to cut her funding unless she kept quiet. They tried to control her. Even after her she was killed by poachers, they continued to profit from her activities.

Passionate individuals are exploited by these big groups. People like Douglas-Hamilton and his work with elephants in Kenya and Biruté Galdikas who worked with the orangutans in Borneo; they are the people who make a difference. Big organizations come in, give them thirteen or so thousand dollars and tell their members that those individuals are working for the organization. They rake in millions of dollars that way. I think it is exploitation, pure and simple.

Today, Kumi Naidoo is at the helm of Greenpeace International. The Executive Director is from South Africa, and he has said that Greenpeace should tackle the problem of world poverty. What does that mean? Is Greenpeace going to become another Red Cross or another Oxfam? Environmental problems cannot be solved by tackling poverty. Environmental problems are creating world poverty, so the environment needs to be protected first. Going about things the other way around just doesn't make any sense. In other words, there simply are not enough resources on the planet to completely eliminate poverty. It is an ongoing battle; we can apply bandages, but that isn't a solution. We have to face the fact that overconsumption of the planet's resources by an expanding human population is at the root of these problems.

You are the youngest of the Greenpeace co-founders; you had just turned eighteen at the time. Your ties to the origins of the NGO are a source of confusion; I have lost count of the number of times we have been asked if Sea Shepherd is like Greenpeace, is a part of Greenpeace or works for Greenpeace. This confusion is a serious handicap for Sea Shepherd because many of the interventions it initiates are erroneously attributed to Greenpeace. It is quite disturbing to see images of Sea Shepherd vessels battling whaling ships in Antarctica and to hear the news announcer say that they are Greenpeace vessels.

Greenpeace has become one of the biggest players in the global good-conscience business. People join in order to feel good, to feel like they are a part of the solution, and so they can say, "I'm an environmentalist, I'm a Greenpeace member, I'm doing my part." That's what they are really selling: a clean conscience.

But in reality Greenpeace is not doing much of anything that is concrete and I think it is a fraudulent organization. They were still collecting millions of dollars to defend the whales and highlighting their fund-raising campaign in aid of the whale hunt in Antarctica in December, at a time when we were sending our vessels there. But they no longer send ships to oppose the whalers. And yet, in the streets, I hear their protesters lying and pretending that the Sea Shepherd vessels are in fact Greenpeace vessels. At least in connection with the dolphins, the whales and the oceans, Greenpeace is a parasitic organization. Millions of dollars are literally being siphoned from the cause in order to perpetuate the bureaucratic machine. It has become a green machine for making money.

I remember when we officially announced our first mission in the Mediterranean in connection with bluefin tuna in the spring of 2010; hundreds of French fishers were afraid that we would sink their boats. There was also some confusion among the fishers because Greenpeace had just blocked a (legal) fishing vessel from leaving port and, simply put, the fishers thought that Sea Shepherd was "… like Greenpeace, but worse." The French secret service came to your conference at Cagnes-sur-Mer, and I had to issue a press release to straighten things up and clarify that Sea Shepherd was only targeting illegal fishing boats.

It is a strategic choice to target only the poachers. It is more difficult and more dangerous, but more effective. I don't really see the benefit of blocking a perfectly legal fishing vessel from leaving port for a few hours, which will in any case leave to go fishing as planned, with fishers aboard who are a little more upset with the "environmentalists." We are interested in concrete results. Destructive but legal fishing must be fought on legal grounds. At sea, we fight the poachers because they are the only ones that we are in a position to stop.

"Charity has always eased the conscience of the rich long before it fills the bellies of the poor."
— Alfred Sauvy (French economist and sociologist)
Mythologie de notre temps

CHAPTER

THE

$\mathscr{C}$HARITY

BUSINESS

Our position was that the more people who were on-site, the better it would be for the whales. I have always been in favor of cooperation between Sea Shepherd and Greenpeace, as soon as they start using the large amounts of funds that they raise in the name of defending the whales — to actually defend the whales.

What happened during that first Sea Shepherd campaign is a good example of the fundamental strategic difference between the two organizations. On June 5, 2010, Greenpeace said that it was trying to free the bluefin tuna from the nets of the tuna seiner the *Jean-Marie-Christian VI*, off Malta. To anyone with a little knowledge of the context, it was clear that the operation would fail to free the tuna and that it would be a media success for Greenpeace.

I see the benefit of drawing media attention to the bluefin tuna problem, but the basic question is, "To what ultimate end?" If the objective is to create the impression that Greenpeace made a sincere effort to free those tuna, that raises some questions. The seiner that was attacked by Greenpeace was a legal one, it was accompanied by other fishing vessels that defended it and the navy was on-site to ensure that the fishing operations were carried out in accordance with the law.

If Greenpeace's real objective was to free the tuna, they would have done things differently. Therefore, the sole purpose was to mount a media event: a Greenpeace activist was seriously injured, two of their Zodiacs were sunk and not one single tuna was freed. But Greenpeace made headlines.

We used a very different strategy. We chose to head for the waters off Libya, specifically because that area is not monitored. No European Commission or ICCAT [International Commission for the Conservation of Atlantic Tunas] vessels venture into Libya to monitor fishing operations. However, it is one of the bluefin tuna's main breeding grounds. And it is also a no man's land with no rules or rights and an Eldorado for any poacher, so it is a priority intervention area for anyone who truly wants to free the tuna.

On June 17, 2010, two days after we entered the Libyan fishing zone, we intercepted two ships, one Italian and one Maltese, that were towing two cages full of bluefin tuna in the direction of a fish farm owned by the Maltese company Fish and Fish Ltd. Contradictory replies to our questions from the fishers, and other factors, made us certain that the tuna in question had not been legally caught. And so, we dispatched some divers who, in the space of 30 minutes or so, cut the nets and freed close to 800 bluefin tuna.

Some people are still convinced that all organizations should close ranks (or at least refrain from disparaging comments) for the sake of the cause. I also was a believer in that appealing moral principle until my first campaign with Sea Shepherd in 2005 in Antarctica. We spent eight weeks aboard our old vessel the *Farley Mowat* hunting down the Japanese whaling fleet inside the sanctuary. I remember that we even had to turn off the heating system in order to save fuel so that we could stay in the area for an additional week. During that time, Greenpeace had raised millions of dollars through a massive fund-raising campaign using the following slogan: "For $30 a month, put Greenpeace between the whales and the harpoons and put an end to the whale hunt in Antarctica once and for all." That year, they stayed at sea long enough to photograph a whale being killed by an explosive-tipped harpoon before returning to port. Later, I saw that the photo was being used in their newsletter to launch another fund-raiser to save the whales. The experience marked a turning point in my view of things, and it was a jarring introduction to the cynical world of some NGOs. Greenpeace is also very critical of Sea Shepherd, and I have seen email messages sent out by local Greenpeace chapters that express real anger about Sea Shepherd's arrival in the Mediterranean for the purpose of intervening in the illegal bluefin tuna fishery. In their opinion, it was their private turf and we were stepping on their toes.

Greenpeace resents Sea Shepherd and me for intervening in the Japanese whale hunt in Antarctica and the illegal bluefin tuna fishery. They are also angry because I exposed their ineffectiveness. In fact, Greenpeace is so angry with me that they posted a message on their website to specify that I was no longer considered to be a founding member. I no longer qualify as an "early member."

And so this group of people who were not present when we founded Greenpeace — many of them had not even been born at that time — are recreating the history of the NGO. By doing so, Greenpeace has turned a page in the old Russian Bolshevik guide to media relations and has simply decided to falsify history. I suppose that in the near future I can expect to be deleted from the official photos dating back to that time.

You left your role as an active member of the Greenpeace organization of your own free will, but you had been excluded from the steering committee prior to that. Why were you excluded?

I was excluded from the steering committee because I had refused to apologize for "an incident" that occurred in Newfoundland during a campaign against hunting baby seals. I had grabbed a sealer's club and thrown it into the sea, together with the skins of the seals he had killed. The Greenpeace office deemed that this was a violation of its principles of "non-violence," and the organization was worried about the bad publicity and financial losses it could create. Another reason for my eviction was my very strong opposition to Patrick Moore, who was up for election as Executive Director of Greenpeace. Moore was opposed to direct intervention. Saving the seals mattered little to him; he was motivated solely by his personal ambitions. I didn't want him to be in control of Greenpeace and I was rebelling, and this was seen as an act of mutiny. I was therefore excluded from the steering committee. Moore took control of Greenpeace and so I decided to leave the organization for good. That same year, I founded Sea Shepherd. That was in 1977.

My concerns proved to be well-founded a few years later. Today, Moore works as a lobbyist and communications person for the forestry, mining, aquaculture and chlorine industries. He was also hired by George W. Bush, the former President of the United States, to promote the nuclear industry. I refer to him as an eco-Judas.

Robert Hunter, the main founder of Greenpeace, a man who had always been a friend and comrade of mine, approved my eviction at the time, even though he said that it was a very difficult decision to make. In the end, he also left the NGO and joined Sea Shepherd as a crew member on our campaigns. His daughter Emily has also participated in many Sea Shepherd missions and today she publicly accuses Greenpeace of being an imposter.[4] My decision to leave Greenpeace was, without a doubt, the best decision I have ever made.

Funding is an important aspect. Greenpeace accuses you of accusing them of having too much money. Their response is, "Greenpeace does not accept money from governments or businesses and our resources are minuscule given the task at hand. We depend almost entirely on donations from individuals."

It is inaccurate to say that Greenpeace has never accepted funding from governments or businesses. My vote was the only dissenting voice on the steering committee in 1976 when Greenpeace accepted a significant donation from Ed Daly of Air America, also known as

CIA Airways. The funding was granted on condition that Greenpeace limit its harassment of whaling fleets to the Soviets while allowing the Japanese to go about their business. That episode marked the starting point of my disagreements with the association's management.

Greenpeace also accepted a significant donation from the Soviet Union in the mid-1980s to sponsor a peace concert in Moscow. I have also noticed that Greenpeace states that it depends "almost entirely" on donations from individuals, which means that there are other sources of funding. But to be clear about my opinion, I do not blame Greenpeace for having too much money; but I do blame them for failing to put it to good use.

Sea Shepherd accepts financial support from some businesses. How do you justify that?

Some businesses have very sincere intentions when it comes to supporting conservation efforts. Companies like Patagonia, Lush and Paul Mitchell, among others, fall into that category. Others support environmental NGOs strictly for public relations purposes. Do those businesses support small organizations and individuals that are not necessarily very well known but that really try to make a difference, or do they contribute only to the organizations that are known and "respected" in order to polish their brand image? Businesses are like people: there are a few good ones and hordes of bad ones. In my opinion, looking at the battles an organization chooses to get involved in can help to determine whether an organization can be considered to be truly independent. Sea Shepherd opposes anyone who violates the laws of marine conservation, and the organization is limited only by our financial resources. Therefore, unless a company is involved in some activity that is destructive for the planet, or has unethical salary policies, we will accept their support. The crucial thing is that no company or individual, regardless of the amount of the donation, will ever be in a position to dictate the limits of our activities, the problems that we can work on or the financial interests that we can attack. Nobody is rich enough to bribe Sea Shepherd. And that is the only form of true independence.

People often get defensive when you criticize Greenpeace.

I believe that our position is a legitimate one. We criticize Greenpeace because they accuse us of being violent and call us ecoterrorists, and also because they attribute some Sea Shepherd victories to their own organization. We also take them to task because they raise funds to combat problems without actually carrying out real campaigns to combat those problems.

What Greenpeace describes as attacks made by the Sea Shepherd organization are nothing more, in reality, than our response to their accusations against us. I do not take accusations of terrorism lightly and I do not agree with the fact that they raise funds to defend the whales in Antarctica without sending any ships there. In my opinion, that amounts to misappropriation of funds. I write to Greenpeace once a year to suggest a conciliation that would allow us to join forces, and they reject my proposal each time. In fact, more often than not, they do not even bother to respond.

Whenever we have been successful in locating the Japanese whaling fleet inside the sanctuary, we have always provided Greenpeace with the coordinates. But they have always refused to do the same. But none of that is of any real importance now, because they have stopped sending their ships to oppose the whale hunt.

A common reaction to the conflict between Sea Shepherd and Greenpeace involves the idea that two organizations that share a common goal should be able to work together instead of becoming entrenched in opposition to each other.

Sea Shepherd and Greenpeace do not share a common goal. We are working toward eradicating the whale hunt, and they are not. Greenpeace supported the recent proposed compromise that would have legalized the Japanese whale hunt (in exchange for putting an end to the whale hunt in Antarctica). The NGO does not oppose the seal hunt in Canada (which was, until the very recent past, the largest massacre of marine mammals in the world), nor does it oppose the massacre of dolphins in Taiji, Japan, or the massacre of pilot whales in the Faroe Islands (the biggest massacre of marine mammals in Europe).

An internal email from Greenpeace France, which was forwarded to me and of which I still have a copy, is a good example of this. The email was written by the person in charge of Greenpeace France's marine campaign and it stipulates that the NGO "will not leave the question of the whale hunt to Sea Shepherd because it is too useful as a tool for raising funds at the international level."

The Greenpeace Foundation, which we created in 1972, has been misappropriated by lawyers, financiers, fund raisers and bureaucrats. It does not in any way resemble our vision of what we were at the outset. Today, Greenpeace earns more money from the whale hunt than the Japanese whaling industry does.

The organization raises millions of dollars to "save the whales," yet their intervention has consisted solely of creating a video game and sending some paper whales to President Obama (the United States already opposes the whale hunt and it is illegal to sell whales in that country). They say that they are working to raise awareness in Japan about the whale-hunting problem, but they are fully aware that only 2% of the Japanese people consume whale meat. In other words, the strategy consists of giving the impression that they are taking action in order to justify their fund-raising efforts, without doing anything significant that could indeed put an end to the hunt. That is precisely why I say that we do not share a common goal. Greenpeace is not an ally of the whales. I call it "the other whaling industry."

But, according to Greenpeace, they are saving the whales in their own way.

They are still using the images of Robert Hunter and myself in the Zodiacs getting in between the harpoons and the whales in 1975 and 1976. They forget that the legacy that allowed Greenpeace to become what it is today was left behind by myself and others who are no longer part of the organization. In fact, none of the founding members of Greenpeace who are still alive today are involved with the organization. We created the tactics that they boast about today, but they have not prevented the death of one single whale. The Japanese whalers have massacred whales under the very eyes of Greenpeace while they were busy flying banners and staging photo shoots. I call that role-playing. And that is why I abandoned those tactics decades ago.

They no longer send ships to the Antarctic, but Greenpeace claims that it is now combating the whale hunt in Japan. For example, on May 15, 2008, they used undercover investigators and testimony from

informants to steal packages containing whale meat. The purpose was to expose the fact that it was being sold on the black market and that it was being sent illegally from the factory whaling ship the *Nisshin Maru*, to the homes of some crew members of that same ship.

It is illegal to hunt whales; therefore the point of exposing the corruption inside an illegal industry escapes me. The whalers are the only people who are hurt by the sale of whale meat. It's akin to the FBI investigating the Mafia on behalf of the don. Stealing parcels of whale meat in Japan has nothing to do with putting an end to illegally hunting whales in Antarctica.

Agreed, but Greenpeace claims to have achieved results. They say that they have "combined a unique trademark made of direct non-violent action, political lobbying, scientific research and public mobilization to put an end to nuclear testing, disposing toxic waste at sea and consolidating the moratorium on commercial whale hunting, along with numerous other steps toward the ultimate goal of a green and peaceful future for our planet."

I have no doubt that Greenpeace has attributed the majority of these successes to itself. There are many devoted and well-intentioned activities in the Greenpeace organization, people who are working on the ground who are inspired by the cause and are doing good things. But I would compare that to the Catholic church. There are thousands of priests and nuns who are devoted and sincere and who work to help the poor all over the world, but they are not the pope. The institution that is the Catholic church is rich, corrupt and powerful, but that doesn't mean that its followers are guilty of the same.

Today, Greenpeace is selling ecological absolution, just like Pope Rodrigo Borgia used to sell divine absolution. It allows people to feel that they are part of the solution without requiring that they change their lifestyle. It is a rapidly growing business. There is an illusion that Greenpeace is achieving results. In some cases it is true, but in reality it looks good but achieves very little. It has become an organization made up of compromises.

"No longer having the strength to act, they talk, discuss, orate, etc."

— Jean Jaurès,
Socialist History of the French Revolution

CHAPTER

A ORLD

OF

APPEARANCES

The captain, a big Norwegian man, burst into the cabin. "What are you trying to do, anyway? Are you trying to get yourself killed? And for what? For a damned seal? It's not worth it, my man. People like you are a menace. To hell with you." And then he left, slamming the door behind him.

Do you think it's possible that Greenpeace and Sea Shepherd could one day form an alliance to defend the oceans?

When Greenpeace was still working in the field, Sea Shepherd would always provide them with the coordinates for the location of the whalers. Our position was that the more people were on-site, the better it would be for the whales. I have always been in favor of cooperation between Sea Shepherd and Greenpeace, as soon as they start using the large amounts of funds that they raise in the name of defending the whales ... to actually defend the whales. As a co-founder of that organization, I must say that I am proud of the ideal that we launched at the beginning of the 1970s, and that we called Greenpeace. Back then we saw it as a revolutionary movement, but that movement is now quite far removed from the bureaucratic corporation that the organization has become today.

The anti-seal hunt campaign in 1977 marked a turning point in the media coverage of the hunt and in my commitment as an activist, because it marked the end of my adventure with Greenpeace.

On that day in March, I was running across the shifting ice toward a sealer who had just split open the head of a baby seal with his club. His arm raised, he was getting ready to kill a second one. Surprised to see me rushing toward him so quickly, he hesitated for a moment, and a moment doesn't last for a very long time. He turned to position his club and he shouted out to me, "This one is for you, you bastard." I grabbed him by the wrist before the club made contact with me. I twisted his wrist so that he had to let it drop, and I kicked the club into the sea. The man was furious, but I was bigger and stronger than him, and so he backed away. I grabbed the little body of the seal he had just killed and brought it over to the sea: "Rest in peace little guy, you will not end up on the back of some witch in Paris." Peter Ballem, the lawyer hired by Greenpeace, came over to me: "You shouldn't do that, Paul. That constitutes theft under the criminal code." In response, I said: "That damned code is not my code."

Together with other members of the team, we had reached the closest sealing vessel, the *Martin Karlsen*. The faces of the sealers lined up on the bridge were covered in blood spatter and contorted with rage. There was a pile of sealskins near the boat and they were tied together and attached to a line connected to a winch aboard the boat. The winch operator was on the bridge and was just about to winch them onboard when I made a lunge for the line. I took a pair of handcuffs out of my pocket and used them to attach myself to it. It was my intent to block the operation, to prevent them from recovering the sealskins. It was a classic non-violent resistance maneuver. RCMP officers were on hand, observing the scene, and I thought that their presence would protect me against any violence on the part of the sealers. I was wrong. In the beginning, the sealers were stupefied and remained silent. Then they started shouting: "Haul him aboard! Haul him aboard!" and "Heave him into the water!" A grizzled old sealer inspected the handcuffs and told me that they were going to hoist me aboard. I kept my confidence. "You wouldn't risk killing me." He sniffled, spat out his chewing tobacco onto the snow-white ice and said, "What risk? We're not gonna risk anything, we're gonna kill ya."

When I felt myself being towed, my heart skipped a beat. I could feel the line getting taut as two dozen sealers aboard the *Martin Karlsen* were shouting words of encouragement to the winch operator. My feet left the ground and I was dragged over the uneven surface of the ice. The RCMP officers were watching the scene, immobile and unresponsive. Suddenly, the ice under my feet gave way and I was plunged into the icy water that soaked into my clothing. In a certain way the shock was a welcome distraction because it meant that I could no longer feel the agonizing pain in my wrist, which was bearing the brunt of my weight. Nor could I feel my twisted leg. But I could feel that I was drowning under a thick layer of melting snow. The winch operator left me there for a moment before hoisting me up into the air again. Then he stopped the machine. I was dangling in the air like a rag doll over the bloody furs. The sealers were leaning over the rail close to me, and were bending down to shout and spit at me. From the ice, Peter Ballem, our lawyer, was shouting something at them. The RCMP guys were still standing there watching us; one of them even broke into a grin. The winch operator started up the winch again and I was once again plunged into the water under the layer of snow. But I couldn't feel the cold any more; I was strangely calm. I had risked my life for what I believed in. *Hoka Hey!*, as the Lakota say. It's a war cry that means, "It's a good day to die." I was in the process of being drowned, and I accepted it.

But the winch operator had something else in mind for me. He hoisted me up into the air again and I started to lose consciousness. I came to again on the bridge of the sealing vessel. A few sealers had dragged me onto the bridge, through the seal blood and grease, and they kicked me and spit on me. They shoved my face into the pile of greasy and bloody sealskins. I could hear some guys screaming out behind me, "Hope ya smother, ya good-for-nothing! Shove the sealskin right down his throat!" Peter Ballem had managed to get aboard and, because he was a lawyer, was able to intimidate the Canadian fisheries officer and convince him to intervene. Peter came and got me and brought me to the captain's cabin. He helped me to get undressed and wrapped me in warm towels.

The captain, a big Norwegian man, burst into the cabin. "What are you trying to do, anyway? Are you trying to get yourself killed? And for what? For a damned seal?! It's not worth it, my man." I was having trouble speaking, but in any case the captain was not in a mood to listen. "People like you are a menace. There have never been as many seals around as there are today. You stopped us from hunting whales and now they're swimming around in the ocean eating all the fish. I was a whaler, now I'm a sealer, and it's your fault. And now you've found another way to get in our way? To hell with you." And then he left, slamming the door behind him.

The following day I started to feel better. My leg was cut up, but didn't require any stitches. I had severe bruising and a number of cracked ribs. I was watching the scene from the bridge. The sealers were scattered over the ice, clubs were being raised left and right and there was blood everywhere. The screams of the seals unable to escape were carried on the wind, filling the air. A fisheries officer came and stood next to me: "You and your gang of faithless, lawless bastards will never put an end to that."

A young sealer approached the boat; he had a writhing baby seal slung over his shoulder. He threw it onto the ice like a sack of potatoes, looked at me and smiled. He gave me the finger and then kicked the seal right in the head. Then he turned it over, and he used his knife to slit it open from one end to the other. With the seal still writhing, the guy put his foot on its head to stop it from moving around and he skinned it. I screamed at him and hurled insults at him. I turned to the officer standing beside me and told him that the man should be arrested because he had violated the regulations of the *Seal Protection Act.* The guy just smiled at me and said, "I don't know what you're talking about; I didn't see anything."

I then left in a helicopter to join another team farther away, in Blanc Sablon. As I was getting out of the chopper, I could see that there were TV cameras and people taking photos. A woman who was bundled up from head to toe came over to me, threw her arms around me and kissed me on each cheek and said, "You're a hero, Paul." I could only see her magnificent eyes, but I didn't recognize her. She kissed me again and then I was taken to the hospital. On the way, I asked Peter who the woman was. He laughed and said, "That was Brigitte Bardot."

Later, I asked her to come with us to the Grand Banks. Her mere presence on the ice that year allowed Brigitte to accomplish more than an entire army of scientists, activists and conservationists. Photos of her that were taken on the Grand Banks as she posed cheek to cheek with a baby seal were seen all over the world. She had already converted the Europeans to the sealing cause. She had even succeeded in influencing the Americans. On March 22, 1977, the American government passed a motion condemning the seal hunt, calling it a "cruel practice." The premier of Newfoundland, Brian Peckford, openly called the motion a "miscarriage of justice." But Peckford could protest all he wanted. In the eyes of the Europeans and the American politicians, he simply could not compete with Miss Bardot's charms.

Covered with bruises and exhausted, I went back to Vancouver. The campaign had been a huge success and even though we had not yet won the war, we had certainly won an important battle. But I had defied Greenpeace management, especially Patrick Moore, so I was expecting to face reprisals back at the office.

I knew that my days at Greenpeace were numbered, but I refused to attempt to rally my office colleagues to my cause, including those who were my friends. If they wanted to squeeze me out because of Patrick Moore (who had sworn that he would fire me), I had no intention of begging.

The meeting that marked the end of my adventure with Greenpeace took place in the home of the organization's accountant, Bill Gannon, newly hired to make Greenpeace a financially prosperous organization.

Moore started the hostilities: "We are a non-violent organization. We cannot allow one of our members to break the law or commit an act of violence. We must be able to fund our upcoming campaigns and we won't be able to do that if we lose our status as a charitable organization and the tax exemptions that go along with it. And we need all of that more than we need you, so I must ask you to resign."

I was furious. "What are you talking about? What violence? I did not attack anyone and I did not damage any private property."

Gary Zimmerman came back with, "Of course you did, you challenged a sealer and then stole and destroyed his property. You threw his seal and his club into the sea."

I was in a state of shock. "But that bastard was about to split open the skull of a baby seal, goddammit. I was not about to just stand there and watch him do it."

Eileen, Patrick Moore's wife, got involved, saying, "We are there strictly to bear witness."

"You are there to bear witness, Eileen, I am there to save lives," I shot back.

Storrow, our new lawyer, intervened: "Paul, I don't think you understand what this organization is about."

I replied, "I am a founding member of this organization. I worked for it as a volunteer for seven years and now a barracuda in a three-piece suit with a hefty salary who had never even heard of us a year ago is telling me that I do not understand what Greenpeace is about?"

Bob Hunter said, "Paul, I understand your point of view, but what you did constitutes an act of violence. We are not asking you to leave Greenpeace. We ask only that you apologize for your actions and that you resign from the executive board. You could come back as a member in a few months."

I was not about to delude myself. "I will never come back as a board member as long as Moore is the executive director. He always said that he would have me kicked out of this organization, and I guess he has finally managed to do it. I saved the life of a seal and I will never apologize for that. I did not injure anyone, and a club is not private property it's an obscenity. And furthermore, I have no intention of resigning."

"Very well, if you refuse to resign we'll fire you! I call for a vote!" shouted Moore.

Only Walrus and John Cormack voted in my favor and that's how I was kicked off the Greenpeace executive board.

Bob also voted to get rid of me, even though he is a long-standing friend. He told me, "Paul, you are welcome to be part of the organization, and you can stay and work with us as an active member."

So I told him, "No, Bob, that's not for me. I will start up my own organization to keep you on your toes, you bunch of bastards, and to remind you of where you came from when you need to be reminded."

Bob laughed because we had already had that conversation, the one about the need to create a Second Foundation, like in the book by Isaac Asimov, in order to monitor the First Foundation and keep it in line.[5] I also knew that, according to Asimov, Greenpeace would always try to discredit and destabilize that second foundation. Sea Shepherd would be an eternal thorn in Greenpeace's side.

While I was getting ready to leave the room, Bob got up to shake my hand. I was told that, after I left the room, he looked the other steering committee members in the eye and said, "Well guys, we've just officially lost our balls." In the end, Bob left Greenpeace in the hands of Patrick Moore and came to work with me at Sea Shepherd.

"There comes a time when protesting is no longer enough; action comes after philosophy."
— Victor Hugo,
Les Misérables

CHAPTER 10

SEA SHEPHERD, UFO ASSOCIATION

Our executive board manages the organization, but during campaigns the captain and the campaign leader have full authority to decide what to do. There are only two guidelines: do not break the law and do not harm anyone. Generally speaking, we never try to achieve unanimity or to conform to the majority opinion.

Some people say that your criticism of Greenpeace is rooted in jealousy and resentment. You are said to be envious of the size of the Greenpeace budget and organization, which are huge in comparison with Sea Shepherd. For example, Greenpeace has 1,500 employees throughout the world, a budget of $300 million and three million members. Sea Shepherd has a mere 30 employees, a budget of $11 million and a hundred thousand members. But, I guess that if your objective had been to achieve the same numbers as Greenpeace, you would have adopted a very different development strategy 35 years ago.

I intentionally rejected all attempts to bureaucratize Sea Shepherd and I have always resisted the fund-raising divas and proposals from people who come to me full of promises: "We will make your organization a super-organization and you will raise millions of dollars because we like what you are doing and we can do the promotion for you." We do not launch massive fund-raising campaigns, we do not send protesters into the streets to recruit donors and we do not do any telephone prospecting to encourage our donors to increase their donations. I have always said that Sea Shepherd will grow by word of mouth. The result is that our support base is more limited, but our members are more loyal because we didn't approach them, they found us. They become members because they like what we do. I think that a thousand Sea Shepherd supporters are worth ten thousand supporters recruited by large NGOs using costly fund-raising campaigns, because our supporters come to us of their own initiative and so they are much more loyal. It is true that the more money an organization has, the stronger that organization is, but that should never be at the expense of passion and imagination. I would never entrust Sea Shepherd to professional donor recruiters. They are like lawyers; they start by telling you what you can and cannot do, and that is a sure road to bureaucratization. In terms of communications, we still have the advantage of having a television series that tells the story of our missions in Antarctica (*Whale Wars* on Animal Planet), and we have grown significantly as a result of the attention the television show has garnered for our activities.

And yet, people seem to think that Sea Shepherd is a much larger organization than it really is. I sometimes get the sense that people expect us to get involved wherever we're needed. I want to ask them, "Do you have any idea of the number of employees we have and the size of the budget we are working with?" Because our organization is involved in relatively spectacular activities and because it intervenes at the international level, people tend to think that ours is a big machine — and that is far from being the case.

Sea Shepherd is only one example of what can be done, and the people who join our organization and support us do so because they identify with what we are doing and they want to contribute to that. The more of them there are, the more support we have and the more interventions we can carry out. We have never been able to conduct as many campaigns simultaneously as we are able to do today, and that's because our support base has grown considerably. That has allowed us to increase our fleet, finance the maintenance and broaden our scope of activities. But Sea Shepherd does not claim that it can save the oceans on its own, and we cannot be expected to get involved wherever we are needed, anywhere in the world. We cannot do it all, because the need is too great. Each and every one of us is responsible for saving the oceans.

And each of us has the ability to do extraordinary things. About 20 years ago, I received a phone call from a man who was living in Glasgow, Scotland. He said to me: "They are killing seals here in the Orkney Islands." So I said to him: "I'm on the other side of the world; what are you going to do about it?" We talked about it for a while, and then he launched a Sea Shepherd group in Scotland. The group went to the island, confronted the sealers and was very enthusiastic and determined. They took the rifles right out of the sealers' hands and threw them into the water. This created such controversy that they were able to raise enough funds to buy the island. Today, it belongs to Sea Shepherd and has become a seal sanctuary. All of that because one man was serious when he asked himself, "What can I do?" If a problem truly affects us, there is a lot that we can do about it.

I remember my first Sea Shepherd campaign seven years ago. I didn't know anything about boats, but when I asked you if I could apply to be a crew member, you said, "If you are ready to work hard and, if necessary, risk your life to save the whales, then, yes, you can come with us."And for me it was the beginning of the adventure, and I am so happy that you did not demand several years of experience at sea in order to take me along! Aside from a few key positions, the crews consist of volunteers who are, for the most part, inexperienced. You have also been criticized for that.

Yes. We are criticized because we take on non-professionals. But if you read the letters that were sent to the editors of the *Times* in 1911, you will find that similar criticisms were made against Sir Ernest Shackleton for that very same reason: he had an inexperienced crew. Shackleton's response to that was, "I don't really want any professionals, I want men with enough passion to get me to the Pole and bring me back alive." And that is exactly the kind of crew that I have, and in 35 years we have not had one serious injury, nor have we harmed anyone. And few sailors can make such a claim. I also find it quite ironic that we are criticized for our lack of experience, because during the years when we were confronting the Japanese whaling fleet in Antarctica there were three deaths, a major fire, an oil spill and more than two dozen accidents with grave injuries on their side. But there were no incidents on our side at all, and yet they are the professionals.

"Are you ready to risk your life to save a whale?" There is no room aboard a Sea Shepherd vessel for anyone who answers that question with a "no." You are also criticized for that.

People think that requiring volunteers to risk their lives to save an animal is asking too much. I have a hard time understanding that. We live in a world where we ask people to risk their lives, die and kill for oil and for control of geographically strategic areas, etc. I think it is much more noble to risk your life to protect a species or a habitat in peril. I cannot think of a better legacy than having contributed to saving a species or a natural habitat. It's simply a matter of a scale of values.

You are still the incarnation of Sea Shepherd. Your opponents say that you are, all of a sudden, some kind of guru. But there is a fundamental difference between Sea Shepherd and a sect because, unlike a sect, people and volunteers are free to join or leave our organization. Why do you think the term is so frequently used by our detractors?

It is well known that all Sea Shepherd members must wear a medallion engraved with my image (laughter)! Demonizing one's opponents with labels is a classic strategy; calling Sea Shepherd a terrorist organization or a sect is not mere slander. The volunteers are free to come and go and they are never asked to do anything against their will. We are an international organization made up of volunteers from the four corners of the earth and they are passionate people who care about the oceans.

Sea Shepherd is still thought of as a radical organization. Don't you think we will have made a major step toward protecting the oceans when its actions are judged not as being extreme, but rather as being the bare minimum?

In my opinion, the butchers are the radicals, the fishers are the radicals, and the people who try to protect the planet are the conservatives. We conserve things; the two words share a common root. It would be difficult to find people who are more conservative. I think that it's important for us to maintain our radical identity, despite the fact that we are a conservation organization. We are fighting to maintain the natural status quo. But attempting to conserve that status quo is a radical concept in an anti-nature society. We will be seen as extremists until the day when passionately defending nature is no longer considered to be a radical idea.

Sea Shepherd is not a democratic organization. Why is that?

In *Star Trek*, Captain James Tiberius Kirk says, "When this ship becomes a democracy, you'll be the first to know." Ships have never been run democratically. There is a captain and a very specific hierarchical structure for the officers and crew members.

Our executive board manages the organization, but during campaigns the captain and the campaign leader have full authority to decide what steps to take. There are only two guidelines to follow: do not break the law and do not harm anyone. Generally speaking, we never try to achieve unanimity or to conform to the majority opinion. That kind of independence of thought and action is essentially anti-democratic, and we fully embrace that. It is what has allowed Sea Shepherd to remain loyal to the spirit of its origins and to prevent compromise from diluting its combative arm. People are free to support us or not support us. To those who disagree with our methods and the battles we choose to fight, I have only one thing to say: "Support another organization because you are not going to change us." It's partly the reason why we will likely never be a very big organization. In order to become one, we would have to make compromises because not everyone would approve of our actions. We made that choice in a very conscious way.

"Our mission involves navigating troubled waters in order to defend the defenseless against those who are unscrupulous."

— Paul Watson

CHAPTER
11

A QUESTION

OF

STRATEGY

We still cling to the idea that we are the center of the ecosystem that we live in, while in reality we are simply one part of it. And when we look at things more closely, we are not even the most important beings. Insects and bacteria rule the world, not the mammals.

Some activists (in ecology, human and animal rights, etc.) feel that we haven't done anything significant because we haven't been found guilty and spent time in prison. This is thought to be a defining measure of effectiveness. In 1971, C.P. Snow, a British writer and scientist, wrote, "When we ponder the dark history of humanity, it becomes clear that many more horrible crimes have been committed in the name of obedience than in the name of rebellion." What is your opinion of civil disobedience?

Civil disobedience has its place. Personally, I do not practice it because I think it does not result in significant contributions, unless it is very carefully planned. However, strategies based on litigation, legislation, education, covert direct action and civil disobedience are all complementary.

I do not think that getting arrested is necessary in order to accomplish something significant. It all depends on the approach. But, if the chosen approach is civil disobedience, then getting arrested becomes a certainty and that brings with it a certain kind of credibility and confidence. I think it would be easier for me to have confidence in an activist who has been arrested than in one who has not.

As regards crime and terrorism, the biggest terrorists are always, and always will be, the politicians. But they are not thought of as terrorists because they are in power.

Japan labeled me an ecological terrorist and placed me on an Interpol "blue notice," but it has not issued a warrant for my arrest. China has registered the Dalai Lama on the same list. So, if the Dalai Lama is a terrorist, I am not going to complain about being in such good company.

Sea Shepherd is an organization that is based on respecting existing laws. Isn't it sometimes tempting to break the law when confronted with something that is legal, but deeply immoral (like massacring seals in Canada, or dolphins in Japan)? What keeps you from going beyond the limits of legality?

The answer is simple: it's a question of strategy. We have to take action within practical limits using all the resources available to us. Breaking the law leads to punishments being levied by the different states. I prefer to frustrate them by brushing up against the line without crossing it. A few years ago, when I delivered a speech at the FBI Academy in Virginia, one agent made the following remark: "The line that separates Sea Shepherd's actions from illegal ones is a very fine one." I replied, "It matters little that the line is a fine one; what matters is that we don't cross it." He couldn't think of a response.

That doesn't exempt Sea Shepherd from being criticized and accused of being a substitute for governments.

We target those who commit crimes on the high seas and we act in accordance with the United Nations World Charter for Nature,[6] which authorizes NGOs and individuals to implement international conservation laws. Sea Shepherd would not exist if the governments of the world had the economic and political will to implement those laws. If all the navies in the world were at sea to protect marine life, instead of playing their stupid naval battle games, we would not have to do their jobs for them. The fact is, they don't care about that in the least, and we are not going to stand back and watch our oceans die without doing something about it. We already have all the laws, regulations and treaties we need to protect the oceans. All of that looks good on paper, and all of the countries in the world agree to sign them, but when it comes to implementing those laws, no one steps up to the plate.

Having the law on your side is clearly an asset. The World Charter for Nature has gotten you out of a tight spot in the past.

Yes. I was arrested in Newfoundland in 1995 for chasing down Cuban and Spanish vessels that were fishing illegally on the Grand Banks. We destroyed their nets and freed their catch, which cost them $40 million. I was brought to trial and was facing two life sentences plus 10 years for having freed their catch. I beat out O.J. Simpson,[7] who was given only two life sentences.

Four weeks into the trial, my lawyer invoked the World Charter for Nature and the jury acquitted me.

Speaking of strategy, Martin Luther King and Mahatma Gandhi are often mentioned as examples of non-violent leaders. What do you think of applying their methods to marine conservation?

"I think that if one day it became necessary to choose between laziness and violence, I would choose violence. I would prefer that India take up arms to defend its honor than to see it become a lazy witness to its dishonor." Gandhi wrote that in *Young India* in 1920. Gandhi's genius was his ability to zero in on the weak point of the English: their sense of righteousness. In this specific case, non-violence was a viable strategy. But it is foolhardy to think that it will work in every case. Gandhi would never have used the same strategy against the Germans or the Russians. A German Gandhi would have been slaughtered by the Nazis.

In reality, we apply the philosophies of Martin Luther King and Gandhi in our actions, with a little bit of Sun Tzu, Miyamoto Musashi and Marshall McLuhan mixed in. I believe in non-violence, which consists of refraining from inflicting any harm on any sentient being whatsoever. Sea Shepherd can indeed destroy private property, but only if the object in question is used illegally to destroy life. I think that a tool, a weapon or any object used to illegally take a life must be sabotaged or destroyed to protect that life. In my opinion, that constitutes an act of non-violence. Any action that that saves a life or prevents attempts to take a life and does not cause any harm to any living being is an act of non-violence.

In 1985, a Tibetan Buddhist monk gave me a little wooden statue and asked me to attach it to our foremast. I thought nothing of it at the time, but I did attach it to the foremast where it stayed for about 10 years. Since 1995, it has been displayed in a prominent place in the wheelhouse of our flagship. In 1989, I had the pleasure of having lunch with the Dalai Lama in Washington. On that day, I learned that he was the one who had given me the little sculpted figurine. I asked him what it represents and he told me that it represents Hayagriva, the symbol of the Buddha's compassionate anger. I didn't really understand what he was getting at. He smiled and said, "You never try to hurt anyone, but when people are not able to see the light, you sometimes need to frighten the life out of them until they do."

When Christians say "you have to give thanks to Jesus, because he died for you," you can reply: "Okay. Jesus died for me, but millions of people died for him, so we're even." You can be very sarcastic when it comes to religion.

People are hairless primates who think they are a divine legend. We live in a world that is dominated by anthropocentric philosophies that tend to make us all believe that humans are at the center of everything. It's as if we were living at the time when Galileo and Copernicus said that the earth was not the center of the universe. We still cling to the idea that we are the center of the ecosystem that we live in, while in reality we are simply one part of it. And when we look at things more closely, we are not even the most important beings. Insects and bacteria rule the world, not the mammals.

All human religions, or at least the ones that I refer to as the "the Divine Monkey religions," adore some kind of giant primate in the sky who tells us to ignore the rest of the natural world. I think that the birth of religion marked the beginning of our contempt for the natural world on which our very lives depend.

But if most people think that animals and nature are there to be exploited by humans, some religions do mention that we should respect nature and condemn the mistreatment of animals.

Yes, perhaps, but if we look at Christianity as an example, St. Paul told people anything and everything. Religion has been used to condemn slavery and to justify it. It can be used to defend nature and as an excuse to exploit it. The bottom line is that humans are still at the center of Creation, and will be no matter what happens. For example, it is no secret that Satan is depicted as a horned creature with hooves and a tail because he is based on Pan, the Greek god of nature. In fact, nature has become Evil, it has become Satan. Satan is just the god of nature in the Christian religion. And we have been waging a war against nature ever since. I have always thought that it is interesting that Christianity claims to be a monotheistic religion. Whenever I ask a Christian: "Who is Satan? He looks a lot like a god to me"; or if I ask: "Who are the angels? You seem to have more gods than the Hindus," I get a puzzled look and the remark: "How dare you say that?" I think that Christianity is just an elevated form of paganism that is no different from the other Greek religions. The Greek gods have all simply become Christian gods. The most interesting one of all is Jesus Christ, who in reality is Hercules. Hercules was born to a virgin. The son of Zeus, he was raised by shepherds in order to be able to serve humanity and his human form ascended to Olympus; the story is exactly the same.

People sometimes tell me that we don't need to worry about "saving the planet" because we are all going to heaven in any case (or to hell if we're bad, I suppose). But everyone will be going to hell because every religion that believes in hell also believe that anyone who is not a believer of that particular religion is going to hell. Therefore, everyone is going to hell because we are all sinners in the eyes of one religion or another.

That is a really good illustration of what a strange species we really are. There is no reference to heaven or hell in the Bible. Neither of the two exists. Hell and heaven were invented centuries ago by two poets, Dante and Milton, and today we believe in those two places.

We invent all kinds of fantasy worlds and people end up believing in them. In a thousand years, people will believe in Jedi Knights. That is precisely the kind of stupid story that gets passed on from generation to generation and that isolates us from the natural world.

You were talking about being concerned that conflict is the main obstacle to action. And the fact that Sea Shepherd does not shy away from confrontation makes it a force to be reckoned with. But that is the very reason why its detractors say it is a violent organization.

We live in a society that values private property more than it values life and that is the real problem. That is why the things we sometimes do are labeled as violence.

But the human race is extremely violent, although some kinds of violence are tolerated while others are condemned.

Imagine that you have just arrived in the city of Mecca and you walk up to the black stone and spit on it. Your chances of getting out of that scenario alive are quite slim, and few people would have any sympathy for you because you would be committing a blasphemous act by attacking an object that a specific group of people hold sacred. People would understand that violence might be perpetrated against you in response to that kind of an act. Try doing the same thing in Jerusalem. Try walking up to the Wailing Wall with a pickaxe and start picking away at the stone; you would not get very far. An Israeli bullet would stop you in your tracks, and people would say that you deserved it because you were attacking something that is sacred to a certain group of people. Or try going to the Vatican and tearing up a photo of the Pope on national television and see what treatment is in store for you.

And yet, people go into the deepest, most mysterious and magnificent cathedrals every day: thousand-year-old forests of giant California Sequoia, the Amazonian rainforest, the forests of the Congo, coral reefs and the fragile depths of the ocean. All over the world, humanity is violating and destroying those cathedrals with bulldozers, chainsaws and trawlers. And how do we react to that? A few people dress up in animal costumes to protest against it while others sign petitions or write to their elected representatives. But if the tropical forests, the oceans and all of the life they contain were valued as much, if they were as sacred to us as an old stone, an old wall or a marble palace in Rome, we would cut the loggers and trawler men up into pieces for their actions. But we don't do it because we are completely alienated from the natural world. Nature is not part of our culture and our life, and we do not understand it.

Humans in general, and governments and corporations in particular, kill when they want something. The United States has killed people in Iraq because they want oil. And you can be sure that they will drill for it in the Arctic National Wildlife Refuge, because as long as there is one drop of oil left on this planet, they will go looking for it. It's a drug and they don't care what they have to destroy or who they have to kill to get it. And no demonstration, no petition, no letter to Congress is going to stop them.

"Anyone who believes that exponential population growth can continue indefinitely in a finite world is either crazy or an economist."

— Kenneth Boulding

CHAPTER
12

AN OVERPOPULATED WORLD

Governments really love meeting to discuss international conservation laws; they concoct resolutions that sound really great, and make a big public display of signing the resolutions and then — nothing. Official photos are taken and they sing their own praises, but nothing substantial ever comes of it.

Most people think that when a law is passed to protect a particular species or habitat, the battle has been won. Isn't that counter-productive in a certain way? Laws that protect wildlife, and marine life in particular, are far from being effectively applied. The fact that they exist on paper gives the public the illusion that the problem has been solved.

Governments really love meeting to discuss international conservation laws; they concoct resolutions that sound really great, and make a big public display of signing the resolutions and then ... nothing. Official photos are taken and they sing their own praises, but nothing substantial ever comes of it.

You are not a big fan of international conferences and meetings on environmental issues.

International conferences never solve anything. There was no follow-up on any of the resolutions passed at the United Nations Conference on the Environment in Rio. It's all just smoke and mirrors. We have had 50 years of conferences and meetings, and the only thing they manage to do is set the date for the next meeting. People love meetings that give them the impression they are accomplishing something. It becomes problematic when the meetings become an end in themselves. People get a warm and fuzzy feeling thinking they are addressing the problem because they are talking about it. Discussing problems becomes more important than solving them. The main obstacle comes from the fact that people are afraid to take action; they are afraid of confrontation. That is why nothing changes.

In 1972, I attended the United Nations Conference on the Human Environment in Stockholm. Young people came from all over the world to listen to our heads of state tell us what we ought to do. They told us that the world was in grave danger and unless we were ready to defend and protect it with a fighting spirit and with passion, there was little hope left. That's what our heads of state told us in 1972. We listened to them, we did exactly what they told us to do, only to be then told that we were too combative and too passionate. And yet, when you look at it, we were not really all that combative.

The main topic of concern at the 1972 conference was the unbridled expansion of the human population. I also attended the

United Nations Conference on the Environment and Development in Rio de Janeiro in 1992. The secretary-general of the conference was a "big ecologist," Maurice Strong, the former CEO of the oil company Petro-Canada. Anyhow, at that time the human population had grown by 1 4 billion people as compared with what it was at the time of the conference in 19/2, and overpopulation wasn't even on the agenda because no one wanted to upset the Vatican or Brazil, the Catholic host country. But the topic was discussed. The greatest threat facing the planet today is the destruction of biodiversity and the extinction of plants and animals. And the engine of that destruction is the unbridled expansion of the human population. So, they decided to discuss the problem while ignoring the cause.

There are now more than 7 billion people living on this planet. You point your finger at overpopulation as the main threat facing the environment. Some see that as an anti-human position and call it a throwback to Malthusianism. But Malthus' approach was different, it seems to me. According to Malthus, anyone who died of hunger simply had no place being born into this world; he thought that famines and epidemics were nothing more than natural selection and that we have to "let nature take its course." In other words, Malthus thought that poor people should simply disappear. How does the ecological approach to overpopulation differ from Malthusianism?

Unlike human laws (and the Malthusian approach), the natural laws of ecology do not discriminate on the basis of race, status or bank account balance. Simply put, there are not enough resources on the planet to feed a human population that is growing and consuming like we are. We are killing the coral reefs, the forests, the wetlands and the oceans. And we are violating the third law of ecology: "There is a limit to population growth because there is a limit to the planet's carrying capacity." We are literally stealing the carrying capacity that could support other species, and that is a violation of the first law of ecology: "The strength of an ecosystem depends on the diversity of the species that make up that ecosystem."

Decreased biodiversity has an impact on everything else; it's the second law of ecology, the law of interdependence. In other words, the increase in the human population is contributing to a decrease in the carrying capacity, and that has an impact on our interactions with other species. It reduces our chance of survival even further and makes a future for us on this earth unlikely. The human population must stabilize itself and if we don't do it voluntarily, nature will look after it for us. Were that to happen, our numbers would be reduced in a very painful manner over which we would have no control. I am not religious, but I think that the four horsemen of the Apocalypse — famines, epidemics, wars and civil strife — will reduce the human population and [bring about] the loss of planetary carrying capacity.

I remember studying population biology at university. The warning signs for the extinction of a species are population explosion, occupation of all available territory and resource reduction. It makes me think that if we want to see a species in danger of extinction, we need only look in the mirror. That leads us to the important question of the decision to have children. Some people who are conscious of how serious the situation really is do not want to have children in order to avoid making things worse.

That's true, but I think that people who are intelligent enough to see it are probably the very people who should be having children, because the vast majority of people who are having children today don't even know why they are doing it. They have kids just because it's the thing to do, because it is expected of them. The result is that there are a lot of children born who grow up without love, education, attention or care, because people don't really think about what they're doing. The anti-abortion movement in the United States is also in favor of the death penalty. But, aside from the inevitable miscarriages of justice, the people who are on death row are, in the opinion of many of us, people who did not receive enough attention and love when they were children because they were unwanted or because their parents were not able to live up to their responsibilities.

The solution I recommend, and for which I have been widely criticized, is that no one should have children unless they have taken a six-month course on responsible parenting and earned a certificate attesting to the fact that they are responsible enough to have children. Today, anyone can have a child, including pedophiles, alcoholics, drug addicts, men who abuse their wives, etc. It is even possible to create one's own victim. That's quite a bizarre situation, if you think about it. A driver's license is required in order to drive a car, a diploma is required in order to access certain types of employment and it is necessary to prove one's ability to do all sorts of things before being authorized to do them. Bringing forth a life is the ultimate responsibility, and people should be able to prove that they are in a position to accept that responsibility. Even if such a measure was not enforced, it would provide people with a different way to learn about what is involved in parenting.

"Whoever controls the media, controls the mind."
— Jim Morrison

CHAPTER

13

THE MEDIA DICTATORSHIP

I think it is impossible to accomplish anything of real significance in this world without creating enemies. I have always looked at the number of people who detest us as a measure of our success. Every time I hear people criticizing us I think that we must be doing something right.

You've met a lot of journalists over the course of your career. What do you think of them, generally speaking?

One of the problems with journalists is that they often claim that they are objective, when there is no such thing as objectivity. Even when people think they are being objective, they can't really do it because everyone has their own priorities. So I think that the first step involves acknowledging that there is no objectivity, while relating the facts as they are and transmitting the information to the best of one's ability. But, acceptance of that fact is not going to sit well with everybody.

In fact, I think it is impossible to accomplish anything of real significance in this world without creating enemies. I have always looked to the number of people who detest us as a measure of our success. Every time I hear people criticizing us I think that we must be doing something right, because I don't think it's possible to be an effective environmental organization without telling people things they don't want to hear and without doing things they don't want us to do. Our job involves upsetting people in order to make them think, shaking up the status quo, rocking the boat and sinking a few, if necessary! It's our reason for being. You could also call us "shit disturbers"!

We want to get people thinking, and the only way to do that is to get their attention. So, to get back to the media, the modern media is the mass media and they understand only four things. Every story carried by the modern media involves one of these four things: sex, scandal, violence and celebrity culture. If a story does not include one of those four elements, it isn't a story and it becomes difficult if not impossible to get the message out. So, you have to tie your story to one of the four elements to ensure that it is picked up and that you get your message out.

For example, in 1984 I led a campaign to protect the wolves in the Yukon, north of British Columbia. The story was perfect; we were making headlines in the media for two weeks. The story involved guys shooting wolves on sight from helicopters, so we had the violence element covered. The same people had threatened to shoot at us, so that added to the element of violence. The Minister of the Environment had accepted a bribe in exchange for authorizing the massacre, so the story also involved political scandal. And we had hired Bo Derek as the spokesperson for the campaign, so celebrity culture was also an element. At the press conference on the story in Vancouver, one of the journalists from the *Vancouver Sun* asked: "But, what does Bo Derek know about wolves? It's stupid; why is she your spokesperson?" I answered: "You are the ones who set the rules for this game, aren't you? If I had shown up with world-renowned wolf biologists, this room would be empty. But our spokesperson is Bo Derek and the room is full; there are 16 TV cameras here and you, all of you, are going to tell this story. It will appear on the front page of your newspaper tomorrow, and there isn't anything you can do to change that, is there? Our campaign created so much media hype that the Minister of the Environment who had accepted the bribe in exchange for authorizing the hunters to shoot the wolves was forced to resign.

When sex, scandal, violence or celebrity culture is involved, you can control communications because the media finds it impossible to ignore stories that involve one of those elements. They are the key to selling newspapers and raising television ratings. People forget that the media is big business. It is no longer a question of informing the people; it is now a question of entertainment. For that reason, when I wanted to launch our television series, I went to see the people at the Discovery Channel and I told them: "Your most popular show today consists of following a bunch of guys around in cold, hostile and remote waters while they catch crabs (*Deadliest Catch*). I can give you men and women from all over the world, in a setting that is even more remote and waters that are colder and even more hostile, with icebergs and penguins. And it's all for a cause: saving the whales. I'll bet you anything that it will be more interesting than catching crabs." It wasn't easy; in the beginning they all rejected the idea. Every producer I met with said the same thing: "Great idea, but it's too risky!" And then Marjorie Kaplan, who was present at the first meeting where I pitched the idea, took over the top job at the Animal Planet channel. She contacted me to say: "OK. We're gonna give it a shot!" And some of the people who watch the show agree with what we're doing, but some of them do not. We have been criticized a great deal by people who say we shouldn't be doing what we're doing. But that doesn't really matter. Thanks to the series, millions of people all over the world know that Japan sends a whaling fleet to Antarctica every year to kill whales inside the whale sanctuary in violation of the international moratorium on whale hunting.

How do you think the media influences our perception of reality?

Everything we do and everything we think is defined and controlled by the media. They are the ones who define our reality. And that is why we are now on a fast track to a collective Darwinian reward: the extinction of our species. The only way to change direction is to understand the kind of trap we have fallen into.

In our media culture, the only thing that matters is having a name. A Hollywood movie about our activities is in the works. When the film is released, no matter which actor plays the role of Paul Watson, I will become a real person for the first time. Because in our media culture, the only people who really exist are the celebrities. In order for an orca to receive protection, it has to have a name like Willy or Keiko, and then millions of dollars are spent. We don't care much about the ones we are not familiar with, but the ones we know must be saved.

A few years ago I got a call from Pierce Brosnan. He said: "Listen, I have to give a speech at a NATO event and I need your help." I asked him why the hell NATO had asked him to give a speech. He said: "They think I'm an expert on the Cold War because I used to play the role of James Bond, and now they want my opinion on it. But I don't know a thing about the Cold War!" So, I wrote his speech for him and I included everything that I think is wrong with NATO, and he read it out word for word. There was a lot of teeth grinding going on that night!

That's how things work in our society; the people with the most credibility are the ones who spend their time pretending to be something they are not.

A few years ago, I was an advisor for the *Captain Planet* cartoon series. I was kept on until the day I made the mistake of actually providing some advice. After that, I was no longer welcome. I was attending a screening of *Captain Planet* at the Environmental Film Festival in Santa Monica. The producer was in attendance and there were about 500 children in the audience; they had come to see *Captain Planet* enforce the law, destroy drift nets, sink fishing boats and save the whales. When the screening was over, the producer asked if anyone had any questions. I raised my hand: "You show Captain Planet getting involved, going to sea and destroying private property to protect life, and I have no problem with that. But why is it that when children who grow into adults do exactly the same things Captain Planet does, your television channel calls them terrorists? Why do you support these activities in the imaginary world and condemn them when they occur in real life?"

The answer is that the media defines our values and our perception of reality.

Your opponents have accused you of manipulating the media. Let's come back to two major controversies. The first one involves the episode in the Antarctic when the Japanese whalers shot at you. Even though the scene was captured on film, some people say that you never provided any proof that the projectile was indeed a bullet and that you lied about it in order to garner media attention.

Those accusations are unfounded. I took the bullet and the vest I was wearing that day to the Australian national police to get the opinion of a ballistics expert. The police refused to provide the expert opinion saying that it fell outside their jurisdiction. I had the bullet examined by an American federal agent who confirmed that the bullet had been fired by a hunting rifle. But the fact remains; I cannot prove that I was shot at and nobody can prove that I was not. There is no jurisdiction in international waters, and that's a problem.

The second controversy involves the *Ady Gil*, the fast interceptor ship used by Sea Shepherd during the 2009–2010 Antarctic campaign. The vessel was cut in two by the harpoon ship the *Shonan Maru 2*. Pete Bethune was the captain of the ship at the time and he was taking part in his first campaign as an activist. He claims that you told him to sink his boat in order to garner public sympathy.

All the proof can be found on our Web site. I did not order Pete Bethune to scuttle the *Ady Gil* after it was rammed. I could not have done it, because it was his boat; he was the owner and the captain and you can see him making the decision himself, on camera. And it was the right decision, a good decision in the opinion of the Australian navy because the *Ady Gil* could not be saved. As for those who think that our goal was to garner sympathy, that is quite simply grotesque. The thing that could certainly have elicited sympathy was the sight of the *Ady Gil* being rammed by a Japanese whaler and cut in two in the middle of the Antarctic with six men aboard. That was the element of the story that people found shocking, not the part about whether or not the boat could be recovered. But if we had been able to save it, we certainly would have. We stood to gain a lot more by keeping the *Ady Gil* than by losing it.

"Propaganda is to a democracy what the bludgeon is to a totalitarian state."

— Noam Chomsky

CHAPTER
14

ECOTERRORISTS

The media is defining our values and our perception of reality. In reality, the ecology movement is the best example of a non-violent movement in the history of social movements. Not one person has been injured, not to mention killed. And yet, in the media we are described as a militia, as ecoterrorists and as extremists.

In 2007, the French diplomat and writer Jean-Christophe Rufin published a novel about ecoterrorism entitled *Le parfum d'Adam*. He was invited to appear on a French TV news and talk show to promote his book. During the interview, he said that the person who had inspired him to write the book was Paul Watson, a man "who does not hesitate to kill innocent people in order to save whales." He looked right into the camera on primetime TV and lied, without batting an eyelid, in order to lend more substance to his book and as justification for the theme of the "threat of ecoterrorism." Rufin describes deep ecology as an anti-humanist philosophy, and in his book the activists who risk their lives to save farm animals abandoned during the war in Kosovo are made to look like potential criminals. According to his logic: "When so little value is placed on one's own life, it is not really possible to value the lives of others." From that starting point, it is no longer problematic to take human lives. Of the sources he claims to have used, Rufin cites an article that appeared in *Libération* on January 30, 2006, which tells the story of fifteen or so eco-activists who were sentenced for ecoterrorism crimes in the United States. A bit of research in the *Libération* archives for 2006 revealed that the "article" to which Rufin makes reference was a mere five lines long![8] It seems that politicians, some intellectuals and some media outlets are making ever larger attempts to manipulate public opinion, demonize ecologists and deep ecology and make them look like violent lunatics and the enemies of humanity.

I'll say it again. The media defines our values and our perception of reality, so someone like Rufin can grandstand on a primetime television show, make false accusations and slander ecologists without being contradicted by anyone. (I was in Antarctica chasing down the Japanese whaling fleet when Rufin publicly accused me of murder on French TV).[9]

In reality, the ecology movement is the best example of a non-violent movement in the global history of social movements. Not one person has been injured, not to mention killed, by an ecologist or a member of an environmental NGO. It simply has never happened. And yet, in the media we are described as a militia, as ecoterrorists and as extremists. But ecologists have been assassinated. Dian Fossey had her skull bashed in in the Congo because she wanted to protect the mountain gorillas. Chico Mendez was assassinated in Brazil because he wanted to protect the Amazon forest. And George Adamson was killed because he wanted to protect the lions in Kenya. The list is a very long one.

So there is an erroneous perception out there involving violence and terrorism, and it is being distilled by public relations firms and politicians; that perception is not based on facts and is unfounded.

Today, the term terrorist is being used to demonize anyone you disagree with. The word is losing its meaning. And as for ecoterrorism, it really means to inflict terror on the natural world.

Why do you think the FBI has listed ecological activism and animal activism as the second biggest threat to national security, after Al-Qaida? Why are governments (and some intellectuals) so afraid of movements that seek to protect nature?

According to the FBI, animal rights movements are an even bigger threat than Al-Qaida. Ecology and animal protection movements are shaking up the status quo even more than is Islam. Our society has centuries of experience with religions. It's a form of mass psychosis that society understands, and religious conflicts are good for business, especially for the arms industry. Ecological and animal protection ideologies are relatively new and pose a bigger threat to the established order and our consumer society than do religious conflicts. Religious beliefs are anthropocentric, for the most part, whereas ecology and to a larger extent animal rights are biocentric. Biocentrism posits that humans are not at the center of Creation, and are not superior to nature. This is a revolutionary idea and a significant threat to the anthropocentric thinking upon which our societies are built.

The establishment fears the tactics of religious terrorists, but knows how to identify them because they are based on anthropocentric values. The animal and planetary rights movements are destabilizing in the sense that they undermine anthropocentric values and that makes them the most significant threat, even though those movements are essentially non-violent. Deep ecology and biocentrism seriously erode the foundation of our economic system specifically because they place life at the center of everything — human life included — while our society values property more than it values life.

And that brings us to the next point, the very fashionable practice of accusing Sea Shepherd members of being ecoterrorists.

Yes. But how is it possible for a terrorist organization to have on its

Board of Advisors the former Environment Ministers for Australia and British Columbia, a former Vice-President of the International Whaling Commission, famous scientists, engineers, artists, writers and actors?

When the Japanese whalers, the Canadian sealers, the Costa Rican shark poachers or the bluefin tuna poachers call us terrorists, I always respond the same way: "Stop what you're doing, or shut your mouth!"

The pathetic practice of constantly labeling as a terrorist anybody who tries, in a non-violent way, to prevent a big brute from clubbing a seal, harpooning a whale or cutting the fins off a shark is simply ridiculous.

But what exactly is ecoterrorism?

There is no law in existence that defines the crime of ecoterrorism. So what kind of crimes do ecoterrorists commit? Setting things on fire? No. Sea Shepherd has never set anything on fire. We don't even allow smoking on board. What about making bombs, planting bombs and throwing bombs? No. We don't do anything like that either. Well, we do throw stink bombs, but they don't explode; they are non-lethal, non-toxic and biodegradable. They just smell really bad. Kidnapping? No. We have never done that, and we have no intention of starting now. And physical aggression is not part of our modus operandi.

People accuse us of throwing stink bombs at the Japanese whalers. Yes, it's true. We have done that. I admit it; I started throwing stink bombs when I was in sixth grade. I confess; I am a recidivist stink-bomb thrower. Having said that, I find it hard to picture Osama bin Laden throwing a stink bomb at a bus full of tourists. And if Timothy McVeigh had used rancid butter instead of ammonium nitrate, countless lives would have been saved.

Sea Shepherd Conservation Society has never done anything to injure or kill anyone. On the contrary; we bend over backward to find ways to intervene that do not harm anyone at all. We don't plant bombs, we don't fly airplanes into buildings, we don't assassinate people and we don't riot in the streets. In fact, Sea Shepherd is such a non-violent organization that neither fish nor meat nor anything that was once a sentient being is served as food on our vessels.

But oddly enough, some fanatical hosts at FOX News, the American TV channel, think that choosing to refrain from eating meat is a sign of terrorism: "My God, you mean you don't eat dead flesh? What kind of a savage are you? You must be a terrorist."

There is a lot of talk in the media about the "butyric acid" thrown at the Japanese whalers by "Sea Shepherd terrorists"... Acid, that must have been really horrible.

Oh yes, the acid. The use of that word conjures up images of steel molting and people with disfigured faces screaming in pain. The truth is, we do use acid in our stink bombs. It is an organic, non-toxic and biodegradable substance called butyric acid. It really does stink, but it is less acidic than beer. I mean we didn't throw lactic acid, citric acid or cola at them, all of which have a higher pH level than butyric acid. The acid in rancid butter is less acidic than milk, orange juice or Coca-Cola, but it smells really bad. It's one of the components in vomit. It is disgusting, but completely harmless. However, the smell is extremely persistent and, if it comes into contact with the decks of the whaling ships, any whale meat that comes into contact with it is spoiled.

But then again, why let the truth spoil such a great story about the horrors of "ecoterrorism"? After all, that's what public relations firms are for. The main mission for most of these businesses is to turn the truth into a lie, and vice-versa, with little regard for reality. What counts, in their opinion, is what people believe to be true.

People are often surprised to learn that the Sea Shepherd organization has never been found guilty of a single crime, despite the fact that for over thirty-five years it has been involved in ramming ships, sinking them while tied up at the wharf and destroying fishing lines and nets.

There is indeed a perception that we break the law, but we are opposed to countries and companies that break the law. And the last place they want to end up is in a courtroom.

In 1986, we sank half of the Icelandic whaling fleet and we destroyed its whale meat–processing plant. A lot of people accused me of being a criminal, but I couldn't find anyone to charge me. I got so frustrated that a year later I went to Reykjavik demanding to be charged. A welcoming committee of 150 police officers was waiting for me at the airport. The head immigration officer asked me: "How long do you intend to remain in Iceland, Captain Watson?" I replied: "I don't know, maybe five minutes, five days or five years. You tell me; I am willing to answer any questions you have." They then brought me to an interrogation room and asked if I would admit to sinking the boats. I said: "Of course I sunk them, and we will sink the other two the first chance we get." The following day, I was escorted to the airport and put on a plane to New York. That morning, the Minister of Justice had said: "Who does he think he is to come here to our country demanding to be arrested ... Get him out of here." The whale hunt was illegal and they knew it. We wanted a trial but we didn't get one, because they know that initiating proceedings against us would amount to putting Iceland on trial.

In 1990, I rammed Japanese vessels that were using drift nets in the North Pacific. Every day, they would put nets in the water that were about 60 miles long, nets that would kill everything in their path; they were also completely illegal. So we rammed them and finally got their attention. At about a thousand miles from the coast, an American Coast Guard plane flew over our head. They told us: "The State Department has just received a complaint that you attacked two Japanese vessels on the high seas." I replied: "That's correct; we also filmed the attack, and we have it here on VHS tape. Tell the State Department we are prepared to cooperate." At 300 miles from the coast, the American Coast Guard officials boarded our vessel and took our statements; I gave them the recording. They told us they would be waiting for us when we arrived in port because we had clearly broken a law, even though at that time they were unable to tell us which one. When we arrived in Seattle, nobody was there to meet us. We never saw them again. After two weeks had gone by, I called the FBI and asked them: "What do we have to do to get arrested around here? What's the problem?" They told me that Japan had withdrawn its complaint. In fact, according to Japan's official version, nothing had happened at all. Even though the video images of the scene had been broadcast on the Japanese news channels, the official line was: "We have not heard anything about such an incident."

At an FBI Academy event two years ago, I delivered a speech. Afterward, one of the agents said to me: "We have files on five hundred of your volunteers, you know. Some of the people who have come through your doors have committed 'eco-crimes.'" I replied: "OK ... and what does that have to do with me?" He said that I had trained those people and that I was therefore responsible for their actions. So, I said to him: "I've got three names for you: Timothy McVeigh, Lee Harvey Oswald and Osama bin Laden. You trained them, so you are responsible."

We get called a lot of things because people just want to demonize us. In reality, everything we do is done in a very overt way. We document our interventions on film. TV crews come to film our campaigns, we appear in public with our faces unmasked and we accept responsibility for everything we do. We give talks to lay out our vision of things and explain our struggle, and we invite the public, the media and even the police to attend these events. I don't think that any terrorist organization does any of those things.

To sum up, I sometimes get the sense that we should perhaps proudly proclaim that we are "ecoterrorists." After all, ecoterrorism is a trend-setting concept with a dark side that I quite like. So it would be just as well for us to embrace this so-called ecoterrorism inside us, this recalcitrant little green devil who can no longer bear to see our planet being divided up and sold to the highest bidder.

"They will continue to be the victims of their own interests until the day that the enormous species ceases to exist."

— Comte de Lacépède,
Histoire naturelle des cétacés

CHAPTER
15

THE ART OF EDUCATING POACHERS

We systematically bring the Japanese whaling industry to the brink of bankruptcy because that is the only thing that will stop them. Things will not change until the nations of the world who signed treaties to protect the oceans order their navies to enforce the laws. Until that happens, we will be that navy; the ocean needs one.

Those who think that Sea Shepherd's actions are too violent or controversial often claim that education is a more suitable solution to environmental problems. They blame us for failing to focus on raising awareness while opting for direct intervention.

In 1979, we tracked down the pirate whaler *Sierra*. All of the "traditional" methods of preventing harm had been tried by different organizations over the course of the previous five years, but without any success. Everyone agreed that the boat had to be stopped, but nobody had managed to do it.

I located it off the Portuguese coast; we rammed it twice and then we sank it while it was tied up in the port of Lisbon. We did not harm anyone in the process, but we did put an end to the celebrated career of the pirate whaling ship once and for all.

When I am told that I should have educated those people instead of doing what we did, I say that sinking the *Sierra* was an educational project.

The harpooner on the *Sierra*, Knut Hustredt, was a Norwegian and, two years later, he appeared on an NBC TV channel in an interview with Priscilla Presley (the wife of Elvis). She asked him what he thought of the people who had destroyed his ship. He answered: "Well, to tell the truth, it was the only way to stop us." She then asked: "But what do you think of the ecoterrorists who deprived you of your livelihood?" He replied: "You know, I never really thought about the whales before that. To me, they were just big fish and that's all. But when I saw that people were willing to go that far, to risk their lives to save them, I started to think about what I was doing. Today, I know that I will never kill another whale, and if Sea Shepherd wants to take me on as a crew member, I am prepared to work with them."

I could educate 450 million Americans to make sure they don't kill any whales, knowing all the while that they wouldn't kill them in any case. But I think that getting a Norwegian harpooner to lay down his harpoon is a much more satisfying educational success.

Even if most of the Japanese people were opposed to hunting whales, that would not necessarily put an end to it. Most Canadians are opposed to the seal hunt, and yet the seals are still being hunted, albeit on a much smaller scale. I think that governments don't really care what people think; their only concern is the interests of corporations.

So we decided to focus on the only two factors they understand:

losses and profits. The only language they understand is the language of economics; everything comes back to economics, it really is key.

I don't think that poachers are aware of the arguments based on conservation or ethics. Money is their only motive. So we try to sink them, economically speaking. From time to time, a whaling ship gets sunk in Norway. Why? To keep their insurance premiums at exorbitant levels; the only way to stop them is to make them pay. Sinking whaling ships that are tied up at the dock forces them to take out war risk insurance, and the premiums for those policies cost up to three times as much as the premiums for traditional insurance policies. We also force them to beef up their security and we make the whole business of the whale hunt less profitable, and that's a significantly dissuasive factor.

Our interventions in the Antarctic have cost the Japanese whaling industry dozens of millions of dollars, and if they had not had access to the funds intended for the victims of the tsunami on March 11, 2011, they would no doubt not have been able to recover from the failure of their last whaling campaign.[10]

By chasing them down and blocking their operations (harpooning and transferring the dead whales to the factory ship) we saved 83 whales in 2006, about 500 in 2007 and 2008, 305 in 2009, 528 in 2010, 863 in 2011 and 768 in 2012.[11] In order to make a profit on the colossal investment that is required to mount an expedition to the Antarctic, they must kill at least 700 whales, and only after that point do they start to make a profit. We have kept them from reaching the break-even point for close to six years.

We systematically bring them to the brink of bankruptcy because that is the only thing that will stop them. Banners, petitions and demonstrations will not silence the explosive-tipped harpoons. And things will not change until the nations of the world who signed treaties to protect the oceans deign to order their navies to enforce the laws that they support on paper. Until that happens, we will be that navy; the ocean needs one.

text continues on page 177

Paul, in 1951. © Sea Shepherd

In June 1975, while Paul was trying to save sperm whales from Soviet whaling ships, an injured sperm whale that had been on the verge of sinking Paul's Zodiac chose instead to spare his life. The experience was to change the course of his life. On that day, Paul came to understand that using himself as a human shield would not be enough to save the whales. © Sea Shepherd

Paul Watson was First Mate aboard the *Greenpeace V* during a confrontation with the Soviet whaling fleet north of Hawaii in1976. © Sea Shepherd

Paul Watson founded Friends of the Wolf in 1984 to protest the authorized shooting of wolves from helicopters in British Columbia. The campaign ended with the resignation of Environment Minister Anthony Brummet, whose actions had been exposed by Watson. © Sea Shepherd

Paul and the only two crew members to remain aboard the Sea Shepherd with him when they rammed the Sierra: Peter Woof (left) and Jerry Doran (right) (1979). © Sea Shepherd

A trapper arrived at a Paul Watson press conference and threw two wolf carcasses on the floor, calling out to Watson, "So, what do you think of that, you bastard?" Watson shot back, "I think you just lost the war, you idiot." (1984). © Sea Shepherd

Paul Watson suggested a non-lethal method for collecting down from baby seals on the ice floes using a brush. Fishers and the Canadian government rejected the proposed alternative (1994). © Sea Shepherd

Paul Watson on the bridge of the *Sea Shepherd* (1996). © Sea Shepherd

The Sea Shepherd vessel *Cleveland Amory* blocks the ramp of a Spanish trawler fishing illegally on the Grand Banks (1983). © Sea Shepherd

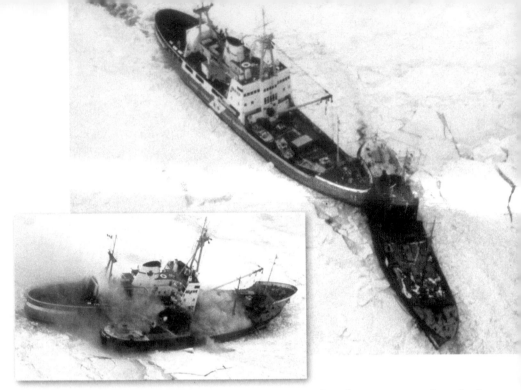

A Canadian Coast Guard vessel rams the *Sea Shepherd II* and boards it after a tear gas attack north of Nova Scotia during an anti-sealing campaign (1983). © Sea Shepherd

Paul Watson and Bobby Hunter attempt to hinder a whaling operation (1975). © Sea Shepherd

Paul Watson and Robert Hunter block the *Arctic Endeavour* by standing in front of it on the Grand Banks (1976). © Sea Shepherd

Paul Watson leads the second Greenpeace anti-sealing campaign on the Labrador coast. He invited Brigitte Bardot to join the expedition to help denounce the massacre. The global media impact of the star's presence was unprecedented (1977). © Sea Shepherd

Marlene Lakin and Cleveland Amory meet with Paul Watson in the New York offices of the Fund for Animals. They helped him to acquire the vessel he used to ram the infamous whaling ship *Sierra* (1979). © Sea Shepherd

Paul Watson meets the Dalai Lama, who gave him an official message of support (1998). © Sea Shepherd

Michelle Yeoh, Pierce Brosnan (a member of the Sea Shepherd Board of Advisors) and Paul Watson at a fund-raising event in Alaska (1988). © Sea Shepherd

Australian Senator Bob Brown greets Paul Watson after he returns from the Antarctic campaign (2010). © Sea Shepherd

The Sea Shepherd crew aboard the *Steve Irwin* before leaving for the Antarctic (2010). © Sea Shepherd

The *Steve Irwin* battles the Roaring Forties en route to the Antarctic whale sanctuary (2011).

Lamya Essemlali, Faroe Islands campaign coordinator, on "spotting" duty with James Brook, manager of the *Steve Irwin* (August 2011). © Sea Shepherd

Transatlantic crossing (2010).

The *Steve Irwin* inside the Antarctic whale sanctuary (2010).

Dolphin massacre on Iki Island, Japan. After negotiating with the fishers for three days, Paul Watson convinced them to put an end to the slaughter (1982). © Sea Shepherd

Sea Shepherd activists attempt to stop the massacre of pilot whales in the Faroe Islands. The Faroese authorities used tear gas and real bullets against the unarmed crew of the *Sea Shepherd II* in an attempt to force them to leave the area. The crew retaliated with water cannons filled with chocolate and lemon pudding. The campaign was the subject of *Black Harvest*, a BBC prime time documentary (1986).
© Sea Shepherd

Annual dolphin massacre in Taiji, Japan. Close to 20,000 dolphins are killed between September and March. Two Sea Shepherd activists spent three weeks in jail in 2003 for having freed 15 or so dolphins (2003). © Sea Shepherd

A female pilot whale and her unborn calf, victims of the massacre near Klaksvik, Faroe Islands (July 2010). © P. Hammarstedt/Sea Shepherd

Female pilot whale and her calf spotted off the Faroe Islands during a campaign to put an end to the massacre. No pilot whales were killed during the six-week-long Sea Shepherd presence. The massacre started up again one week after the Sea Shepherd vessels left the area (August 2011). © Sea Shepherd

Pilot whales massacred in the vicinity of Leynar, Faroe Islands. Between 1,000 and 1,500 pilot whales are killed in the Faroe Islands every year; it is the largest massacre of marine mammals in Europe (August 2010). © Sea Shepherd

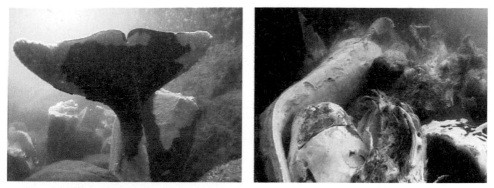

Underwater pile of pilot whale carcasses discovered during the Sea Shepherd–Fondation Bardot mission. © F.X. Pelletier/Sea Shepherd (August 2010)

Sea Shepherd crews recover illegal fishing lines from the sea. © Sea Shepherd

Sea Shepherd activists throw bottles of rancid butter onto the deck of a Japanese factory whaling ship inside the Antarctic whaling sanctuary. © Sea Shepherd

A Sea Shepherd vessel is confronted by a Canadian Coast Guard vessel (right) and a sealing vessel (left). Anti-sealing campaign 2005. © Sea Shepherd

Sean O'Hearn, former Director of Sea Shepherd Galápagos, with fins from sharks that were illegally killed inside the marine reserve. About 20,000 sharks are poached inside the reserve every year. © Sea Shepherd

Japanese Coast Guard officers hurl stun grenades at Sea Shepherd crew members inside the Antarctic whale sanctuary. © Sea Shepherd

The *Shonan Maru 2*, one of three Japanese harpoon ships, moments before ramming the *Ady Gil* (2010). © Sea Shepherd

Sea Shepherd activists prepare to foul the propeller of one of the three harpoon ships of the Japanese whaling fleet inside the Antarctic whale sanctuary (2012).
© Photos: Sea Shepherd

A Sea Shepherd activist prepares a rope to be used to foul the propeller of a Japanese harpooner (2012). © Sea Shepherd

A Sea Shepherd activist prepares to hurl red paint, symbolizing whale blood, onto the deck of a Japanese factory ship. © Sea Shepherd

The *Steve Irwin* follows closely behind a Japanese factory ship inside the Antarctic whale sanctuary to prevent it from hoisting whales up the stern ramp (2011). © Sea Shepherd

The *Ady Gil*, cut in two as a result of the impact with the *Shonan Maru 2*. © Sea Shepherd

The *Gojira*, the fast trimaran that replaced the *Ady Gil*. It has since been renamed the *Brigitte Bardot*. ©
Sea Shepherd

An operation to free bluefin tuna in Libyan waters (June 2010). © Sea Shepherd

Some of the 800 illegally caught bluefin tuna destined for Fish and Fish, the Maltese fish farm. They were freed by Sea Shepherd activists on June 17, 2012. © Sea Shepherd

A Sea Shepherd activist cuts the net around cages full of bluefin tuna. The cages are 90 feet deep and 150 feet in diameter. © Sea Shepherd

The *Isba II*. Sea Shepherd sank this Spanish pirate whaler in the port of Vigo. Its sister ship, the *Isba I*, was sunk on the same day (April 1980). © Sea Shepherd

Two of the four Icelandic whaling ships sunk by Sea Shepherd activists who also destroyed the whale meat–processing plant, all of which cost the Icelandic whaling industry some $10 million. It took 16 years for the industry to recover (November 1986). © Sea Shepherd

The whale meat–processing plant destroyed by Sea Shepherd activists in Hvalfjordur, Iceland (November 1986). © Sea Shepherd

On July 16, 1979, Paul Watson twice rammed the famous pirate whaler *Sierra* just outside the port of Leixões. The impact created a crack in the hull above the waterline, causing $1 million in damage. Sea Shepherd put an end to the career of the whaling ship once and for all by sinking it in the port of Porto on February 6, 1980. © Sea Shepherd

A Sea Shepherd activist sprays indelible organic dye on the fur of a baby seal in order to ruin its commercial value. Watson and his team used this method to save close to a thousand baby seals before being arrested (March 1982). © Sea Shepherd

Until quite recently, the Canadian seal hunt was the largest massacre of marine mammals in the world. © Sea Shepherd

Watson fought for over 30 years to put an end to the massacre. © Sea Shepherd

Sharks poached from the waters off Cocos Island. © Sea Shepherd

Diver François Sarrano swimming off Mexico alongside a 15-foot female great white shark; he describes the moment as one of the most beautiful he has ever experienced. © Galatéefilms Oceans

Protesters gather to protest Germany's arrest and potential extradition of Paul Watson on May 23, 2012
©Paul McKinnon / Shutterstock.com

Paul Watson and Lamya Essemlali at a public event in Paris (April 2011). © Franck Langel

A young audience member listens closely while Captain Paul Watson speaks in Paris (April 2011).
© www.bonpiedbonoeil.net

It seems quite clear that it was not an awareness-raising campaign that has prevented the Japanese whaling fleet from killing its quota of one thousand whales in the Antarctic, year after year. It was the direct result of Sea Shepherd's interventions, and one piece of evidence in support of that, among others, comes from a classified American State Department document that was released by WikiLeaks to the Spanish newspaper *El Pais* in January 2011. In that document, the Assistant Executive Director of the Japanese Fisheries Agency, Mr. Yamashita, clearly states: "In recent years, harassment from the Sea Shepherd Conservation Society has prevented the Japanese whaling fleet from catching its quota of whales." WikiLeaks also revealed that Japan was secretly pressuring the American government to revoke the organization's charitable status (and the tax deductions that go with it). An update on the discussions between high-level government authorities — namely Japanese government representatives and the US Secretary of State, Hillary Clinton — for the purpose of bankrupting an organization involved in protecting the oceans, has made this a very embarrassing situation for both governments.

For us, the best part of the document is Japan's admission that Sea Shepherd had in fact prevented it from catching its quota in recent years. That statement itself confirms that our interventions are effective. As regards our charitable status, Sea Shepherd has not broken one single American law and so the American government has no valid reason to take action against an American organization and American citizens, simply because it would please Japan. This year, Japan also tried to use an American court to prohibit our interventions in the Antarctic, but Judge Richard A. Jones threw out the injunction, saying that there is a notable difference between what Sea Shepherd was doing and what the Somali pirates were doing, namely the use of AK-47s (the comparison had been made by the lawyer for the whalers). The judge even added that he would be giving some thought to the reasons why Sea Shepherd was intervening in the Antarctic. In other words, despite itself, Japan had just drawn even more attention to what it was doing in the whale sanctuary. Japan has also tried to turn against us the countries that support Sea Shepherd in one way or another.

Japan is one of the most powerful countries in the world, and that makes our battle against their illegal whale hunting in the Antarctic all the more difficult and lengthy. Only a country as powerful as Japan could intentionally ram a ship and sink it in the middle of the Antarctic Ocean, narrowly missing killing the people on board, without having to answer for anything to anyone. Japan is directing increasing levels of violence at us. They spend millions of dollars developing offensive and defensive tactics to use against us. They cover their ships with protective netting, they attack us using Long Range Acoustic Devices (military devices) and high-pressure water cannons; they also fire golf balls at us. I was wondering where all the golf balls on board the ship were coming from. Then we found out that they bring thousands of them with them to the Antarctic. They amuse themselves by throwing them off the aft deck. They do this in a sanctuary, an area that is covered under the Antarctic Treaty. Throwing thousands of golf balls into the sea is a violation of that treaty. Every year, they also throw several thousand tons of whale grease, flesh and blood over the side, also in violation of the treaty. Under the pretext of "scientific research," Japan targets endangered whale species in an established whale sanctuary in violation of the international moratorium on whale hunting, in opposition to the Australian federal court, in violation of the Convention on International Trade in Endangered Species of Wild Fauna and Flora and the Antarctic Treaty. These people are criminals.

But they have a lot of power. They put pressure on any country that allows us to fly its flag, because no ship can take to the sea without flying a flag. We have lost the right to fly the flag of Canada, Belize, England, Togo and many other countries. We are currently flying the Dutch flag, since Holland has no right to withdraw its flag from any ship registered in that country. As an example of Japan's power to influence other countries, Holland is now trying to pass special legislation for the sole purpose of being able to withdraw its flag.

We also have another flag that only our ships are entitled to fly. It is the flag of the Five Iroquois Nations. They gave us their flag when they saw that other countries were refusing to allow us to fly theirs. Unfortunately, the Iroquois flag is not recognized by other governments, but it is still the one that we take the greatest pride in flying.

Japan also had you listed on the Interpol blue notice, apparently because it wants to be kept up-to-date on your every movement. It was quite strange to see your Facebook status updated every time you took a plane, and to see your special note for Japan: "No need for the Interpol notice, you can just follow me on Facebook!" Did being listed with Interpol have an impact on your life?

The main impact for me, was the fact that it saved me from the interminable waiting lines at international airports! When I would return to the United States by way of Canada, a security agent would come up to me and ask me to follow him. I would say: "What's the problem? Japan, again?" And the guy would answer: "Yes. They have filed a complaint against you." But it's odd because all the security agents I have encountered at the border were fans of *Whale Wars*,[12] so they were all really friendly. I would ask them: "OK, what is it this time?" And they would say: "Well, Japan is accusing you of ecoterrorism." "Does that mean that I'm going to be heading to Guantánamo?" But it was just a question of following the usual protocol, doing a bit of paper work and then I was free to go. I remember one security agent who, after having searched our bags, said in a very friendly way as we were leaving: "Hey, you guys, why don't you use torpedoes?" Well, for obvious reasons ... (Laughter).

Strangely enough, one of the first insults hurled at Sea Shepherd has been co-opted by the organization and is now a part of its identity: the pirate flag.

Our detractors started to call us pirates over twenty years ago. So, I said to myself: "OK. We will be pirates, but pirates of a different kind. We will be compassionate pirates and we will go after the pirates who are motivated by greed and profit." That makes real sense to me. In order to understand it, you have to go back to the seventeenth century, when piracy was out of control in the Caribbean. The British navy was not doing very much to stop it because a lot of the proceeds from piracy were being passed along in the form of bribes. So piracy flourished until one man put an end to the festivities: the pirate Henry Morgan. Piracy was brought to an end by a pirate, not by any government. Governments are the biggest pirates of them all. Other pirate do-gooders include Jean Lafitte, who stood up to Andrew Jackson in an attempt to defend New Orleans in 1814, and John Paul Jones, who founded the American and Russian navies some 200 years ago. Pirates know how to get the job done without letting bureaucracy get in the way, and that's how we see the work that we do. But we have our own code of honor. The Sea Shepherd code of honor prohibits injuring or killing our enemies and dictates that we act within the framework of the international conservation laws. While at sea, we oppose only the illegal exploitation of marine life.

"He who pillages a small boat is called a pirate, while he who pillages a large ship is called a conqueror."

— Greek Proverb

CHAPTER
16

THE BIGGEST
*P*IRATES
OF THEM ALL

And one more type of plunder must be added to the illegal fishing practiced by rich countries. For a long time, local fishers have been accusing European vessels of dumping their toxic and radioactive waste in the waters around Somalia, and those accusations have been confirmed in a UN report.

Let's talk about pirates of a different kind. The first time I heard about the piracy in Somalia, I was watching the news on TV. A French tuna boat had been attacked by pirates, and the French fishers were saying it was scandalous and unjust not to have safe, normal working conditions. They were demanding that the French navy come to their defense. I remember wondering what the French fishing boats were doing in the waters of one of the poorest countries in the world.

The biggest pirates in Somalia are not the Somalis. When compared with the big pirates like the French, Spanish, Japanese, Americans, Taiwanese, and Russians, the Somalis are mere small fry.

Somalia has one of the longest coastlines in continental Africa: 2,000 miles of the most fertile waters in the world. While 80% of the world's fish stocks[13] are being overfished or have already collapsed, the waters off Somalia still support some species that command a very high price on the global market, including tuna, sardines, mackerel, lobster and shark.

When the civil war brought the last government to its knees in 1991, those territorial waters became — according to Peter Lehr, a lecturer on terrorism at Scottish universities — "an Eldorado for fishing fleets from many different nations." Since that time, the waters off Somalia have been pillaged by fishing fleets from industrialized countries.

A United Nations report published in 2005[14] estimates that at least 700 industrial fishing vessels were fishing illegally in Somali territorial waters, in that year alone. We destroyed our own "fisheries resources" through overfishing, and now we are attacking theirs. Over $300 million worth of tuna, shrimp, lobster and other species are stolen from Somalia every year by the huge foreign trawlers that invade these unprotected waters. In reference to the piracy in Somalia, Peter Lehr has said: " ... It's akin to a kind of trade; the Somalis recover about $100 million per year in piracy ransom while the Europeans and the Asians poach about $300 million worth of fish from Somali waters every year."

In addition, those rogue fishing fleets have no interest whatsoever in the conservation of fishing zones that are not inside their own territorial waters. They use fishing methods that are prohibited in their home countries, methods that are among the most destructive in existence — and all for one single purpose: to take as much as possible as quickly as possible. It can be compared to shoppers who find themselves in a giant superstore with no cashiers or employees of any kind. But the goods available to be looted are marine life forms. And that is why, while most of the population struggles to survive, Somali fish are being sold in the fish shops of the richer countries. It's understandable that the situation is creating some degree of frustration along the Somalian coast.

And one more type of plunder must be added to the illegal fishing practiced by rich countries. For a long time, local fishers have been accusing European vessels of dumping their toxic and radioactive waste in Somalian waters, and those accusations have been confirmed in a UN report.[15] Nick Nuttall, of the UN Environment Program, has stated that "Somalia has been used as a dump site for hazardous waste since the beginning of the 1990s and it has been going on since the civil war began." He also reports that a European company found that it was advantageous to illegally dump its hazardous waste. At a cost of $2.50 per ton, as compared with $1,000 per ton to treat the same waste in Europe, it's not hard to understand why.

As a result of the tsunami in 2004, a large quantity of waste washed up on local beaches, making the local population ill. That waste is only the tip of the iceberg. Millions of containers are strewn along the coast and, when erosion caused by the sea action breaks open those containers, some of which are already leaking, an unprecedented humanitarian and ecological catastrophe will hit the area. Generally speaking, the simplistic version of the situation involving the Somali pirates presented by the media, the one according to which the pirates are vulgar mercenaries drawn to the prospect of easy money and jealous of the opulence that passes by so close to their shores, seems to be somewhat partisan, to say the least.

Once again, the media defines our reality, tells us what to think and identifies the good guys and the bad guys for us. Before taking up arms and becoming pirates, the Somalis tried to alert the international community and asked the United Nations to take action. The United Nations turned a deaf ear and buried its own reports on the situation. It seems that the UN hears only what it wants to hear, based on the origins of the complaint. Even though it ignored the Somali cries for help, the UN did respond positively to the nations whose fishing fleets were being attacked, Spain and France for the most part, and authorized a military intervention in the area by those countries. They were later joined by others, including the United States, China, Japan and even India.

The Somali pirates were initially motivated by a desire to protect their waters and their livelihood. In a country where there is absolutely no protection from the greed of unscrupulous rich countries that take advantage of the situation, the pirates declared themselves to be the "Volunteer Somali Coast Guard or Navy."

In a country where the population is on its knees, it quickly became apparent that piracy is a profitable activity. When warlords started getting involved and sharing the loot with the pirates, the foreign fishing fleets were no longer the only targets. The fact remains that piracy is supported by most of the Somali people because they also benefit from the ransom money. And that is a significant factor, and understandably so, in a country where 73% of the population lives on less than two dollars a day.

I do not condone the activities of the Somali pirates, but a desperate situation calls for desperate measures. All of it could have been avoided if the international community had not ignored the calls for help. Instead, foreign fishing boats are now fishing illegally under the protection of the military from their own countries. These rich nations continue to steal from one of the poorest countries in the world, and they are using the taxpayers' money to do it.

When they were holding hostage the *Faina*, a Ukrainian cargo ship loaded with arms, the pirates were surrounded by American navy ships. Their spokesperson, Sugule Ali, responded to Jeffrey Gettleman from the *New York Times*, who had asked him if he was afraid: "No, we are not afraid. We are ready. We are not afraid because we know that death comes only once." I think a movement that recruits people who are that desperate — and therefore determined — has a certain kind of invincibility, because people who have nothing left have nothing to lose.

A military crackdown is not the answer, especially if it is directed exclusively at the Somali pirates and ignores — or indeed protects — the causes of the piracy. Somalia is just the beginning; the phenomenon will spread to other African countries whose waters are also being illegally fished out and used as dump sites for rich countries. After Somalia, we will see a similar situation in Ivory Coast, Nigeria, Congo, Benin, Senegal, Guinea-Bissau, Mauritania and other countries. In 2001 alone, 600,000 tons of toxic and radioactive waste from rich countries were dumped in the waters off the African coast. Justice must be meted out in this area; otherwise there will be no peace and the situation in Africa will explode. When it comes to growing terrorism, injustice is the most fertile ground.

Apparently, some governments still have a significant interest in modern piracy. For example, Sea Shepherd faces significant corruption in the Galápagos (a UNESCO World Heritage Site).

In the Galápagos, corruption is even more evident, because we work in partnership with the police. It's odd to see that almost all police officers sport our pirate logo on their radios and their bags. The police force is not the problem in the Galápagos; the navy, which is much more corrupt, is the problem. The poachers can take advantage of the situation because Marine Reserve guardians must provide the navy with their patrol itineraries in advance. The navy then informs the poachers, and that makes it very easy for them to avoid the patrols. To get around that problem, we often get "lost." We also frequently have "trouble with our compass," and as a result, we stray from our planned itinerary and end up finding the poachers. When that happens, the navy can't really say too much about it.

Having said that, it's still a real challenge. In January 2007, the President of Ecuador awarded me the Amazon Peace Prize, and in August he had my Director of Operations arrested in the Galápagos because he had arrested one of the President's friends. So, there are still high points and low points!

Costa Rica is also a good example of government corruption. That story was touched on in *Sharkwater*, a documentary about the shark fin fishery. The producer, Rob Stewart, had taken part in Sea Shepherd's anti-poaching campaign in 2005, for film-making purposes.

That shark campaign in Costa Rica really revealed the extent of the corruption inside Abel Pacheco's government; it was being directly influenced by the Taiwanese government. Subsequent events also confirmed all of our allegations: the Taiwanese had deposited $11 million into Pacheco's Panamanian bank account. While we were patrolling the waters off Costa Rica, we came across a Taiwanese vessel that was fishing illegally for sharks, so we informed the Coast Guard. Claudio Pacheco, the President's brother, was the head of the Coast Guard, and he was quite frank with us. He said: "If the vessel is flying the Taiwanese flag, we cannot do a thing about it." He added that we could take photos if we wanted to, but the Coast Guard would not raise a finger to stop the Taiwanese. In the end, Claudio Pacheco lost his position because he was trying to do his job properly.

Costa Rica has a reputation for being a conservation-minded country. But in reality, it has the worst record in Central America when it comes to the shark fin fishery. The destruction of Cocos Island, an area where sharks congregate off Costa Rica, is a real tragedy. The rangers are doing their best, but they don't have any equipment and they don't get any support from the government. We had cameras and forty-five witnesses aboard when we confronted the fishers from Costa Rica. They didn't have any cameras, and they accused us of trying to kill them. We produced our evidence before the court in Punta Arenas and their complaint was dismissed. Then they appealed that decision. The case was handled by a different judge and prosecutor, and once again it was dismissed. Two weeks later, they told me that I would be arrested, because in Costa Rica people can go to jail for up to a year while an investigation is being conducted. I told them that I had no intention of playing that game, so we hoisted our sails and left port, with the Coast Guard on our tail. One year later, I called to find out what was happening with the investigation. They said that the investigation would not be getting under way until I had been arrested and put in prison. Later, the judge presiding over the case told me that he could wind things up if I gave him $100,000. I refused, of course.

"When the government violates the rights of the people, insurrection is ... the most sacred of rights and the most indispensable of duties."

— Article XXXV
of the *Declaration of the Rights of Man and the Citizen, 1793*

CHAPTER

17

A FEW WORDS ABOUT GOVERNMENTS

What happened in the Gulf oil spill is a scandal, an unforgivable crime and a flagrant demonstration of the fact that the oil companies can do whatever they choose, when they choose, to whomever they choose without having to worry about the consequences.

You often say that governments don't solve problems and they are, in fact, always part of the problem. But people count on governments for that very thing; they expect them to solve problems.

And that is the problem. Our dependence on governments has created one disaster after another. Governments do not solve problems, they create them. Problems are always solved by the courage, imagination and passion of individuals, and that is the way it has always been. Contrary to what we have been told, slavery in England and in the United States was not abolished by any government, nor did the government give women the right to vote. Those victories are the fruits of the efforts made by individuals like William Wilberforce,[16] Frederick Douglass[17] and Susan B. Anthony.[18] All social revolutions are conducted by individuals like Gandhi, King, Aung San Suu Kyi[19] and Mandela. In terms of conservation, people like Dian Fossey, Jane Goodall, Brigitte Bardot and Steve Irwin, to name a few, are the ones who are making a difference. Individuals conduct social and philosophical revolutions, and politicians take credit for them. For example, President Woodrow Wilson is credited with having given women the right to vote when he signed the 19th amendment to the United States Constitution. But in reality, he fought the suffragettes and persecuted them right up until the time of their victory. With a few rare exceptions, politicians are nothing but parasites.

To get to the point where it is possible to make really significant decisions, a person must undergo an invisible vetting process. I was discussing that with Martin Sheen, who is a member of our Board of Advisors. I asked him: "Martin, why don't you run for President of the United States? After all, lots of people already think that you are." Martin is not stupid. He said: "You know, if I were to do that, I would have to stoop down in order to get through the door of the Oval Office, because whoever becomes President of the United States, Prime Minister of Canada or President of France is pre-determined long before the people cast their ballots. They are chosen long enough in advance to give us the illusion that the citizens are the ones who elect these people. But it's nothing more than an illusion."

Isn't there any way to force governments to keep the promises they make to the people who elect them?

There should be a law that stipulates that any politician who fails to keep an election promise can be fired. They should be charged with fraud and deceiving the public.

What do you think of the progress that the Green Party has made in many countries?

I really do not have any political leanings, in the usual sense of the term. My views do not align with the left-wing, the right-wing or the center. As a biocentrist, my politics necessarily include all of life, including plants and animals.

I met Petra Kelly in the early 1980s, and I was one of the first members of the Green Party of Canada. I even ran as a candidate for the Greens in the Vancouver municipal elections. I left the party when it started adopting left-wing, politically correct positions that went against positions that I deemed to be ecologically correct.

In theory, I think the idea of a Green Party is a good one. But in practice, it seems to be corrupted by anthropocentric values, to the point where we have a Green Party in Germany that is supporting the war in Afghanistan.

Noam Chomsky has said: "The more powerful the group, the more support it lends to the politicians who serve its interests." You often say that the United States is controlled by the oil companies. The British Petroleum (BP) oil spill in the Gulf of Mexico is the biggest case of marine pollution in all of history. How does that catastrophe show that corporations control the politicians?

I refer to the United States as an oilocracy, because it is governed by and for the oil companies. George W. Bush and Barack Obama are for the oil companies, and that was clear for all to see when the oil spill occurred in the Gulf of Mexico. There were very few consequences for BP, and it controlled the politics of the situation. We were prohibited from getting involved, but we were allowed to try to save the animals that were covered in oil.

What happened in the Gulf is a scandal, an unforgivable crime and a flagrant demonstration of the fact that the oil companies can do whatever they choose, when they choose, to whomever they choose without having to worry about the consequences.

The Obama Administration folded when confronted by the industry. Today, it is still giving out permits to oil companies that want to drill in the Gulf, including BP.

Many dolphins, whales, turtles and birds, not to mention millions of fish and invertebrates, perished. After the disaster, BP spread astronomical quantities of dispersants — their own product — in an attempt to dissolve the oil. These compounds are very toxic and fatal for the Gulf ecosystem. And BP made money on it.

A few years ago, Scott West, an agent for the American Environmental Protection Agency — he now works with Sea Shepherd — had gathered enough evidence to send the Executive Director of BP to prison, because he was responsible for a pipeline leak that caused a spill of close to 10 million liters of oil in Alaska. The federal prosecutor called the agent to a meeting to tell him that the case was closed. West replied that a case could not be closed while the investigation was still under way, but the Bush administration decided to bury the case because BP had agreed to pay $20 million in fines. The corruption that made it possible for BP to buy impunity in Alaska is also the cause of the disaster in the Gulf of Mexico. It could have been avoided if the government had done its job.

Americans believe they live in a democracy, but they are governed by the oil companies. And it's not a new phenomenon. It started in the 19th century, when whale oil was still being used. Then in 1917, Prohibition came into effect because the oil companies realized that farmers could manufacture their own fuel using fermented apples. In the 1890s, ethanol was the fuel being used in automobiles, agricultural equipment and locomotives. And in 1919, the Prohibition police destroyed the corn alcohol distilleries farmers were using to produce their own ethanol fuel, which forced them to turn to gas.

In a certain way, we are all responsible, as individuals and as an organization. Sea Shepherd's detractors often point to the fact that our vessels use a lot of fuel. And they are right about that, even if I tend to think that that is the best was of using it: to stop poachers from killing marine life. In my opinion, that is a much more noble way to use fuel than the millions of ships that use astronomical quantities of it for the purpose of war or trade.

It is true that Sea Shepherd uses fuel, and we also use lubricating oil. Unfortunately, the whalers, the sealers and those who fish illegally force us to use fuel. And so, we depend on it just as much as anyone else.

Today, despite the situation with climate change due to greenhouse gas emissions, we continue to drill for oil. And once we have exhausted all of the reserves outside the boundaries of protected areas, we will start drilling inside national parks and world heritage sites.

Oil has caused wars, conflicts and ecological disasters and that will continue to be the case. Oil companies will continue to destroy lives (human and animal) and wreak havoc on natural ecosystems with impunity because we haven't found a better alternative with which to grease the palms of our politicians.

The president of the United States serves the oil companies first, then the citizens; the environment is last in line. And that is the case with heads of state all over the world. All presidents and prime ministers, members of Congress and Parliament serve the oil industry.

At least Donald Trump was honest enough to admit that the wars currently being waged by the United States in the name of democracy and human rights are in fact motivated solely by oil.

We are going to have to find alternatives, and until that happens we will have to limit our use of oil to absolute necessities. Other sources of energy will have to be found for transportation.

But above all, we need a new vision. We must find the will and the motivation to liberate ourselves from our deadly dependence on oil.

"Nothing will benefit human health and increase the chances for survival of life on earth as much as the evolution to a vegetarian diet."

— Albert Einstein

CHAPTER
18

YOU ARE
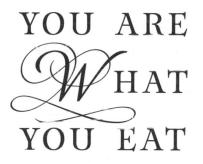
WHAT
YOU EAT

In reality, fish have a much larger role to play in our survival by being present in the oceans than by being served up on someone's plate. Fish act as the natural glue that keeps marine ecosystems in place. They ensure that the oceans continue to function. If the fish disappear, the oceans will die.

As individuals, what we choose to put on our plates (or leave off our plates) can have the biggest impact on the earth. Which, of course, brings us to the question of veganism, because Sea Shepherd vessels have been serving a strictly vegan[20] menu for many years. You say that Sea Shepherd does not actively preach veganism, even though an animal rights organization could well do so, but the fact that our vessels serve a vegan-only menu does indeed send a strong message.

We serve only vegan food on our vessels because I do not think that anyone who claims to be an ecologist should be eating meat. Veganism is the answer to many environmental problems. For example, a vegan who drives a four-wheel-drive vehicle every day contributes fewer greenhouse gas emissions than an omnivore who rides a bicycle, because the meat industry produces more greenhouse gas emissions than the automobile industry. It takes 13,500 liters of water to produce one kilogram of beef, and 80% of the deforestation in the Amazon rainforest is done to make room for livestock. That is the real "inconvenient truth" that Al Gore fails to mention in his documentary. That might be because he owns ranches in the United States.

Eating meat is contradictory for anyone who defends the oceans. More than 40% of the fish caught are used as food in the livestock and aquaculture industries.

Mackerel in the North Atlantic are dying of hunger because we are fishing the sand eels they normally eat in order to provide a source of food for intensive poultry farms in Denmark. Domestic cats eat more tuna than do all the seals in the world combined: 2.5 million tons of fish are fed to domestic cats every year and, when you think about it, it is a strange situation because if a cat were to encounter a tuna in nature, the tuna would eat the cat. As for fish farms, that is not a solution either: seventy-five wild fish have to be caught in order to raise one fish in a fish farm. We are literally devouring the oceans.

What we choose to eat or refrain from eating is a more decisive factor than any other thing. But people are generally very reluctant to make radical changes to their eating habits.

I grew up in a fishing village, so I was raised on a diet consisting almost exclusively of fish and seafood. Today, I simply could not live like that because I am aware of the consequences. We are literally stripping the oceans of its fish. If I can live without eating fish, then anyone can do it. It's simply a question of being concerned enough to take that step. And it's not as difficult as it might seem; vegan food is largely underestimated by omnivores. It is a diet that is rich in delicious food, unlike the sad and boring image of it held by some people.

Whalers often compare eating whale meat to eating farm animals, and they use this argument to justify hunting whales: "Some people eat pigs; we eat whales and dolphins."

I don't condone the slaughter of farm animals. Our ships serve an exclusively vegan diet and we promote vegetarian diets for ecological and ethical reasons.

That being said, the method used to kill the whales — or the dolphins in Taiji, for example — would never be tolerated in an abattoir. It takes anywhere from ten to forty-five minutes for the whale to die after being hit by an explosive-tipped harpoon. And sometimes the weapon is not sufficient to do the job; sometimes the whales try to flee, in which case firearms are used to "finish them off." Half of the females killed in the Antarctic are pregnant. Those methods would not be tolerated at any abattoir anywhere in the world. In other words, they would be illegal.

In addition, whales are a protected and endangered species, whereas that is not the case for cows and pigs. Whales are part of an ecosystem and they contribute to making that ecosystem function properly, and again, that is not the case for cows and pigs. I am not saying that people should eat cows and pigs; I am saying that they should choose to refrain from eating them for other reasons. It always exasperates me when people make that comparison in order to justify hunting whales, especially when the Japanese do it, because we know that they eat more pigs, cows and chickens than Australians and New Zealanders combined. Whale meat is eaten by only 1% of the Japanese people; most of the population eats farm animals, so the analogy is completely grotesque.

Most people (scientists, journalists and the general public) use the term "stock" or "fisheries resources" when talking about fish. They use the term "tons" to quantify them. That says a lot about our perception of them ... We would never think of talking about "tons of elephants" or "tons of dogs."

We talk about tons of fish. But fish are individual, conscious creatures; they are all unique. They are at least as important as the animals that live on dry land. Everyone would be shocked, to say the least, if we were to criss-cross Africa shooting giraffes, lions, elephants and monkeys on sight, from a helicopter. They would also be shocked if we were to use half of the meat to feed our farm animals and pets, while leaving the rest — the species that we don't want — to rot in the sun. But that sort of thing happens every day with impunity in every sea and in every ocean in proportions that defy comprehension. Today, less than 0.01% of the surface of the oceans is protected from fishing activities. The most frequently fished populations have been reduced by 90% as compared with fifty years ago. We are pushing all the limits, fishing in ever-deeper waters for fish that are smaller and smaller while using technology that is more and more sophisticated. Today's fishing techniques involve using satellites to find fish that can try to flee but have nowhere to hide. In terms of numbers, there is no massacre anywhere on earth to compare with the massacre of fish. People pay little attention to their suffering and that is reflected in the language we use when we talk about "stocks" and "tons." We have such little regard for them that people who claim to be vegetarians continue to eat fish without thinking that it is in the least bit contradictory.

But in reality, fish have a much larger role to play in our survival by being present in the oceans than by being served up on someone's plate. Fish act as the natural glue that keeps marine ecosystems in place. They ensure that the oceans continue to function. If the fish disappear, the oceans will die.

By destroying the fish, humanity is committing suicide. And that is what is happening right now. A United Nations study forecasted that the world's commercial fish stocks will crash by 2048 — in other words, tomorrow morning. That will put a definitive end to the festivities for humanity. And yet, people don't seem to find it all that alarming. We still want to eat fish and don't seem to care that the individual fish are getting smaller and smaller while the price goes higher and higher. People don't know how to interpret these signs of an impending disaster.

We should not be eating fish. There are simply too many of us. Nobody can legitimately claim to be a marine ecologist and conservationist while continuing to eat fish. It is the ultimate form of hypocrisy.

More and more reports are telling us that there are toxins in the fish we eat. For example, a recent study showed that the high levels of mercury present in many fish can cause serious neurological disorders such as Alzheimer's disease. This is quite ironic given that fish is generally thought to be a good choice for combating Alzheimer's, due to the Omega-3 fatty acid content. Do you think that, ultimately, the thing that will save the fish from humanity's boundless gluttony is the fact that we have poisoned them?

I don't think it will have any impact, because nobody is thinking about it. In the United States, for example, the labels on cans of tuna bear the following warning: "Not to be consumed by children and pregnant women"; this is due to the high levels of mercury. So basically, the government is saying: "Too bad for you if you are not a child or a pregnant woman, but we have to sell this stuff to somebody!"

Near Los Angeles, on a jetty in Santa Monica there are warning signs in English, Spanish and Vietnamese. They all say the same thing: "Don't eat the fish; they contain toxins." And every day you can see a hundred or so people fishing there. People don't care. They are consciously ingesting poison.

And there are a few public relations firms out there who are very effective in terms of making us feel comfortable with the idea that the level of poison is acceptable. We are filling the sea and the air with poison, and we carry on as if there were nothing wrong. Japan just officially increased the acceptable level of mercury; it is now double what it used to be. A few years ago, Sarah Palin claimed that a little bit of radioactivity is good for your health. But then again, Palin is a good example of what happens when you eat too much mercury.

"We are still surrounded by people who think that what they have been doing ... can go on indefinitely."

— David Brower

CHAPTER
19

SUSTAINABLE DEVELOPMENT IS A *B*USINESS LIKE ANY OTHER

There are 7 billion human beings living on this earth, so the equation is a simple one: there are too many people and not enough fish. Therefore, if we really want to eat fish, there is only one way that we can do it sustainably. People would have to use a fishing rod to catch their own.

The term "sustainable development" is very popular right now. What do you think of that concept? Isn't it a bit of a contradiction in terms?

I think the term was coined by a former Prime Minister of Norway, Gro Harlem Brundtland, at the Rio Conference on the Environment in 1992. It has come to be a synonym for the idea of "business as usual." It is a myth that was invented in order to justify more development, with some good conscience added in.

Let's talk about what's known as "a sustainable fishery." I have never quite understood the concept of a color-coded guide to "sustainable consumption" (green = OK, orange = to be avoided and red = prohibited). You have to admit that, while people refer to these guides for "responsible" fish consumption and purchase fish on the green list, that green list will become the red list in less time than it takes to say it aloud.

When a fish is sold in Paris, New York or Tokyo and it is identified as catch from a "sustainable fishery," that's a lie.

Our problem is that we do not think of individual fishes; instead, we think of "fish" in general. We don't think about what they actually are. It takes a salmon four years to grow, reach sexual maturity and die. An orange roughy does not reach sexual maturity for forty-five years and can live for up to 200 years, like the cod fish. These species might not survive human exploitation. There are 7 billion human beings living on this earth, so the equation is a simple one: there are too many people and not enough fish. Therefore, if we really want to eat fish, there is only way that we can do it sustainably. People would have to use a fishing rod to catch their own. I think that is a more sustainable solution than these so-called guides to responsible consumption.

Do you think that all of the fisheries in the world should be closed?

We should be doing what the Polynesians used to do, namely declare any areas that have been overfished to be "off-limits areas." The Polynesians would refrain from fishing those areas for ten, twenty or fifty years depending on the rarity and life cycle of the fish species. They were very strict, because anyone who dared to fish in an off-limits area would be sentenced to death! These prohibitions were taken very seriously because the future survival of the community depended on respecting those off-limits areas. I think that the entire Mediterranean should be declared an off-limits area for at least thirty years in order to allow it to recover. However, the problem is that there is more than one problem area and, at the global level, the illegal fishing industry is bigger than the legal one. Nothing has been put in place to ensure that the laws are enforced and marine life is protected.

The area of ocean being trawled every year is fifty times larger than the area that is subjected to deforestation, and yet not many people get upset about it. The fact that what is happening at sea is not visible to the general public makes it more difficult to get people interested in protecting the oceans. How can we get around that problem?

It is a real challenge. Humans are terrestrial creatures who live their lives on dry land and who, for the most part, have absolutely no connection to the marine world. They do not see what is happening at sea and so it does not have an impact on hearts and minds. If terrestrial animals were treated the same way we treat marine animals, it simply would not be tolerated. Over the course of the last fifty years, a movement to educate the public and raise awareness has attempted to change things. The movement was initiated by Captain Jacques-Yves Cousteau, together with others such as Dr. David Suzuki, Sir Richard Attenborough and the French director Jacques Perrin.

And yet, changing that mentality has been a slow and difficult process. We are in a race against time and there seems to be no sign on the horizon of a radical change in the average person's habits. And it seems to me that contenting ourselves with eating organic food and buying the fish that appear on the "green list" amounts to little more than spitting on a burning house. A revolution in eating habits is not just around the corner.

We are not visionaries; we have a very short-term collective memory, and that is a problem. We need to look the future in the face and start applying the lessons learned from past mistakes. One of the things that stops us from doing it is our incredible ability to adapt to the deteriorating living conditions on this earth.

For example, years ago there were a lot of belugas along the East Coast of the United States; there were polar bears, known locally as white bears, in Vermont and New Hampshire. There were walrus in Maine and on the coast of Nova Scotia, in Canada. Other species have become extinct over the past couple of centuries: the eastern bison, the Carolina parakeet, the Labrador duck, the Newfoundland wolf, the sea mink, the giant penguin, the Atlantic gray whale, the right whale ... I could go on and on. We pushed all of these species into extinction and, in our collective memory, it is as if they had never even existed. The biosphere is being destroyed, little by little, and we're getting used to it.

If we were to go back in time to 1965, and if I were to say: "Forty years from now, water will be sold in bottles and we will pay more for it than we now pay for gasoline," you would no doubt think that I was insane, and would probably tell me that nobody will ever pay for water. Since that time, we have gotten used to the fact that living conditions on earth have deteriorated.

We have already exterminated 90% of the fish. The fish population is 90% smaller than it was before we began to wage war on the oceans.

In the fishing village where I grew up, it was easy to spot the poor children: they would come to school with a lobster sandwich every day. The turbot that we saw for sale in a Paris fish shop the other day, being sold for about $16 per pound, was thought of as "garbage fish" twenty years ago. Nobody would eat it — it has absolutely no taste. But once again, we adapt to impoverished conditions. When one species of fish is lost, we move on to another one. I used to joke about it by saying that at that rhythm, we would soon be reduced to eating jellyfish. And then, I attended an event in Vancouver where jellyfish salad was being served.

And now, guides to sustainable consumption are being promoted and "eco-labels" are supposed to tell us how we can all continue to eat fish responsibly. Nobody wants to make any radical changes. Instead, we try to convince ourselves that we can continue to eat fish, because we now have "sustainable fisheries." But there is no such thing as a sustainable fishery that can feed 7 billion people. That idea is nothing more than an illusion. And yet we want to believe it because we have an incredible capacity to adapt to the deteriorating condition of the planet. We have a short memory span and we are completely disconnected from the natural world. We are maintaining a state of collective denial that is going to destroy us.

"Earth provides enough to satisfy every man's need, but not every man's greed."

— Gandhi

CHAPTER
20

THE TRAGEDY OF THE COMMONS

When the Norwegian industrial fishing fleets arrived in the waters off the coast of India, they took everything. One million independent Indian fishers lost their jobs. These industrial fleets are the real pirates and they are using government subsidies — taxpayers' money — to make a handful of individuals rich while destroying the oceans.

In 1968, an article entitled "The Tragedy of the Commons" was published in *Science*. In that article, the ecologist Garrett Hardin unequivocally describes the vicious and suicidal process that led humanity to practice overfishing to the point where we could literally empty out the oceans, right down to the last fish. He explains that when a shared and limited resource is exploited by different entities that are each pursuing their own personal interests, all of them tend to maximize their profit and little thought is given to sustainability. That continues until the shared resource is completely destroyed, because the logic is that of "whatever I don't take will just be taken by someone else." That is precisely what is happening to the marine life in the oceans, especially far out at sea.

The oceans are in the process of dying and protecting them should be the number one priority of navies all over the world. But instead, they play stupid naval battle games. The American Navy kills many dolphins and whales when they test the sonar used to locate enemy submarines ... They continue to spend astronomical sums of money on equipment that is totally useless ... Al-Qaida doesn't have any submarines! They are destroying nature instead of protecting it. At the same time, governments are propping up commercial fisheries with subsidies of more than $10 billion per year. And the largest fisheries, and therefore the most destructive ones, are the ones that get the biggest subsidies.[21]

The most ecologically destructive activity on the planet today is fishing. Why? Because fishers are now in a position to destroy life on this planet as we know it.

When the government of Canada looks at the ecosystem on the East Coast of Canada it sees three things: seals, fish and fishers. But one thousand species that are connected to each other in a very complex way make up the food chain of that ecosystem, and each time one species is removed from the chain the entire system becomes more fragile.

What happened with the cod in Newfoundland is a good (and sad) example of what you are talking about ... The sealers are former cod fishers who are saying that the seals are responsible for the collapse of the cod stocks in 1992. They claim that killing the seals will allow the cod to recover.

There used to be about 50 million seals in the waters off Eastern Canada, or ten times as many as there are today. And there had never been any problems with the cod stocks; cod was abundant for thousands of years, right up until the advent of industrial fishing. The cod stocks collapsed due to the greed of the Canadian government and the profound incompetence and disastrous approach to management practiced by Fisheries and Oceans Canada.

In reality, if we want more cod we have to have more seals, not fewer seals. The ecosystem in the North West Atlantic is rich in biodiversity, and the interaction between the different species maintains the ecological equilibrium. Only 3% of the seal's diet consists of cod. Seals feed mainly on fish species that feed on cod, so reducing the numbers of seals decreases the cod's predators and therefore increases the number of cod. Although human beings are by far the biggest predators of cod.[22]

The decision to support the seal hunt was ostensibly based on that fallacious argument, but in reality it was motivated not by science but by political interests. The politicians in Ottawa want to avoid, at any cost, having the fishers pointing their fingers at the incompetence of the Department of Fisheries and Oceans. They needed a scapegoat, and seals fit the bill. Brian Tobin, the former Minister of Fisheries and Oceans, said that the seals were responsible for declining cod stocks. He said what the fishers wanted to hear and went against the findings of his own department.

In January 2012, one bluefin tuna was sold at auction in Tokyo for $736,000. One single fish. The media relayed the information with the relish usually reserved for athletes who break records. None of the major media outlets mentioned the disastrous significance of such an amount. You refer to the bluefin tuna fishery in the Mediterranean as the "extinction economy." How is that fishery different from what we have known up until the present time?

Most commercial fisheries in the world are in the process of collapsing, but the bluefin tuna is special because it is the most expensive fish in the world. Because of that, the motivation to fish as much of it as possible is much stronger, as this can beef up short-term profits. The bluefin is a warm-blooded creature capable of attaining speeds of up to 50 miles per hour in just a few seconds. It is the fastest fish in the world and one of the most fascinating that has ever populated the ocean. And today, it is in danger of extinction. But instead of trying to save it, a company like Mitsubishi is buying as much as possible. Rarity creates value and that translates into the highest prices for the thousand bluefin tuna they have stored in their enormous walk-in coolers. Today, the average price of a bluefin tuna is in the neighborhood of $700,000. When the tuna disappears, a few years from now, Mitsubishi will be the only company selling it. The company is in a position to meet the demand for about fifteen to twenty years. And being the exclusive source (together with a handful of other companies), it will be in a position to set the price, which means that it will make billions of dollars in profits. Firms like Mitsubishi are not fishers. When the bluefin tuna disappears, they will simply move on to some other moneymaker. The oceans are being plundered by companies that don't care about the future of the fishery. Their strategy involves the short-term maximization of profits. Even though Sea Shepherd does not support any fishery, we do differentiate between those that want their children to be able to go fishing and those that simply want to empty out the oceans so they can become the exclusive owner of one species after it becomes extinct in its natural habitat.

Bluefin tuna have no chance of surviving if drastic conservation measures and the means to enforce restrictions on fishing are not put in place.

Many famous chefs are getting involved and are refusing to serve bluefin tuna or swordfish, for example, but I don't think anyone should be eating fish any more. We should really give them a break.

Sea Shepherd has been concerned about the bluefin tuna problem for a long time, and in 2010, the organization was finally able to raise enough funds to launch an intervention in the Mediterranean. It was a success, because on June 17, 2010, Sea Shepherd cut the lines to a cage full of tuna in Libyan waters, freeing close to 800 bluefin tuna that had been illegally caught. The tuna were to be sent to Fish and Fish Company, the Maltese fish farm. It is interesting to note that even though the Maltese government accused Sea Shepherd of damaging the country's economy, the move was applauded by traditional Maltese fishers.

Yes. In fact, in an article entitled "Malta's traditional fishermen salute Sea Shepherd,"[23] Charles Bugeja, a fourth generation fisher, stated: "The Sea Shepherd activists are doing what the government should have done to protect the bluefin tuna and the livelihood of traditional fishers who for many generations have made a living from fishing the seas."

The ecology movement is not the enemy of small independent fishers. Their real enemy is industrial fishing, an industry which tries to pass itself off in the media and in the eyes of the public as a "normal" fishery, but it is not a normal fishery. Bugeja was right when he said the following, in reference to the tuna seiners and fish farms like Fish and Fish: "These people are not fishers, they are businessmen."

When the Norwegian industrial fishing fleets arrived in the waters off the coast of India, they took everything. One million independent Indian fishers lost their jobs. And even though there is no talk of that in the press, we do hear about ecologists interfering with the fishers. In the meantime, these industrial fleets are the real pirates because they are using government subsidies, also known as the taxpayers' money, to make a handful of individuals rich, to the detriment of the fishers. They are the pirates that we want to stop in their tracks.

"It is clear that the quantity of bluefin tuna that end up at fish farms is not being monitored."
— Excerpt from *Thon rouge,*
quota et survie de l'espèce,
Montpellier SupAgro, March 2008

CHAPTER
21

TOO PRECIOUS TO BE SAVED

We act under the auspices of the United Nations World Charter for Nature, which gives all legitimate citizens and the NGOs the right to enforce the environmental laws (within the limits of the law — when the "competent" authorities are incompetent). And that is very clearly the case with bluefin tuna.

Sea Shepherd is now being sued by Fish and Fish, the company that is farming wild bluefin tuna, the same company that had intentions of farming the 800 bluefin tuna that were freed from their nets by Sea Shepherd in June of 2010. They argue that it doesn't matter whether the tuna were caught illegally or not; what matters is that Sea Shepherd should not have freed them. That position is a good example of the feeling of impunity that is typical of this industry.

They have every reason to feel confident. In March of 2010, the Convention on International Trade in Endangered Species of Wild Fauna and Flora (CITES) refused to place bluefin tuna on the list of species for which there is a prohibition on international trade. During that same year, CITES did not list any of the marine species recommended for a prohibition in international trade, and that had never happened before. Five species of shark, two species of coral and the polar bear were rejected. The porbeagle shark was already on the list, but it was removed.

Criteria that are purely economical and political have prevented these species from being protected, and, regarding the bluefin tuna, there is significant pressure, especially from Japan, Libya and China.

In other words, science is no longer the decisive criterion; economics, culture and politics are now determining whether a species is protected or not. When it was announced that bluefin tuna would not be exempt from international trade, the Japanese delegation stood up and clapped. In concrete terms, CITES will protect wild species from international trade only in cases where that trade is not too lucrative. The organization has lost all relevance and credibility. It has been bought out.

After that move by CITES in March of 2010, all eyes looked to the International Commission for the Conservation of Atlantic Tunas (ICCAT), which met in Paris the following November to set the bluefin tuna quotas for the 2011 season. As in previous years, ICCAT again ignored all of the scientific recommendations (and good sense) and authorized a fishery between May 15 and June 15, or at the height of the reproductive cycle, on the very grounds where the tuna reproduce (which is unheard of for terrestrial species). But all those tuna spawning at the same time on the surface of the water are much easier to catch. And that has become the prevailing criterion: ease of capture.

In the end, ICCAT authorized a quota of 12,900 tons (or about

1.29 million tuna),[24] as compared with 13,500 tons (or 1.35 million tuna) in 2009. The quota for 2010 was set in accordance with a "salvage" plan for the species which should, according to its authors, allow bluefin tuna populations to recover by 2020, with a 60% likelihood of success. But then, who in their right mind would choose to fly in an airplane that had only a 60% chance of reaching its destination without crashing?

It is also important to note that those figures are valid in the absence of illegal fishing. But in 2010, roughly 141% of the quota was illegally caught, or about 1.5 million tuna.[25] And yet, ICCAT doesn't seem to be losing any sleep over it. But what else are we to expect from an organization that is nothing more than a consortium of countries that fish bluefin tuna? It's akin to asking hunters to set their own quotas and hunting season dates, monitor the hunt and set the fines for infractions.

CITES, ICCAT and the European Commission do not really want to take the steps required to save the bluefin tuna. There is simply too much money at stake.

In 2006, scientists recommended a quota of 12,000 tons (1.2 million tuna). The ICCAT decided to set the quota at 32,000 tons (or 3.2 million tuna). In the end, 60,000 tons (or 6 million tuna) were caught that year. That would never be tolerated with regard to terrestrial animals. The bluefin tuna is a warmblooded animal; it is an extremely fast-swimming predator, the leopard of the oceans. But at the average price of $700,000 per tuna, it's not enough to be the fastest fish in the ocean — that won't help them escape from human greed. The bluefin tuna is on the same sad path as that of the Newfoundland cod.

During Sea Shepherd's 2011 bluefin tuna campaign, Simon Busuttil, the Maltese national spokesperson and a member of the European Parliament, made the following statement in reference to Sea Shepherd's activities: "We did not mandate any NGOs to carry out inspections. If that happens, fishers must report these illegal activities immediately so that we can take the necessary steps. Inspections are carried out exclusively by the authorities from the European Union Member States, and not by anyone else." Such a defensive attitude on the part of the monitoring organizations would not be so disturbing if they were doing their job. But they do not seem to be putting much effort into their work, because the bluefin tuna population in the Mediterranean has dropped by close to 85% since 1970. A quick look at the illegal fishing figures is all that is needed to justify giving these so-called monitoring bodies a score of zero. But, as Simon Busuttil failed to mention, the bluefin tuna does not belong to ICCAT or to any of the "authorities of the European Union Member States," and their flagrant incompetence is detrimental for all of humanity.

Simon Busuttil is right about at least one thing: Sea Shepherd was not mandated by the European Union or by ICCAT. If those organizations had any real intention of putting an end to poaching and saving the bluefin tuna, we would know about it. We act under the auspices of the United Nations World Charter for Nature, which gives all legitimate citizens and NGOs the right to enforce the environmental laws (within the limits of the law) when the "competent" authorities are incompetent. And that is very clearly the case with bluefin tuna: a few greedy industries are subsidized and protected by their governments, incompetent and corrupt monitoring bodies and relatively indifferent citizens. An excellent recipe for extinction.

" ... it is a custom more honored in the breach than the observance."

— William Shakespeare,
Hamlet

TRADITION, OR THE ART OF JUSTIFYING THE UNJUSTIFIABLE

The human species is extremely destructive. I find these stories about traditions to be extremely exasperating; anything that involves killing an endangered species or destroying a natural habitat under the pretext of tradition is unacceptable. Ecology must take precedence over tradition.

There is one argument that is often used to justify all kinds of massacres. It is a concept that consists of saying that it is acceptable to do anything simply because it has always been done, while ignoring the need to change in a given context. I am talking about "tradition." Japan, Norway, the Faroe Islands and the Makah all use tradition as justification for massacring whales ... What is your position on "traditional hunting"?

Tradition is no excuse for breaking the law. Norway and Iceland are violating the international law on conservation. They are killing whales even though an international moratorium on commercial whaling is in place. The Japanese can invoke tradition as much as they like, but Japanese whaling only began in 1947 when General MacArthur set up their whaling fleet. So it wasn't a Japanese initiative; it was an American initiative for Japan. As for the Makah people, they were also violating the law. The Makah had not hunted whales since 1920, when the commercial hunt had almost completely wiped out the whale population. But the tribe announced that they were going to start hunting whales again when the gray whale was taken off the list of endangered species in 1994. They claimed that their right to kill whales was rooted in their culture, but if that is the case shouldn't we also be authorizing the Haida people to kill the Makah? It's a part of their culture. The Haida believe that when they die, their souls are reincarnated as whales, and the Makah kill whales. So, are the Haida entitled to kill the Makah for cultural reasons? Where do we draw the line? Should some cultures, but not others, be authorized to kill whales? The law authorizes the Inuit to hunt a few whales, but this requires an uninterrupted tradition and it must be necessary, for subsistence purposes. The Makah do not meet either of those criteria. The Makah had planned to create a commercial partnership with the Japanese and Norwegian whaling industries, which held great promise for access to lucrative markets. In fact, many of the Makah were opposed to getting involved in the whale hunt, which was supported by only a handful of elite families. When we got involved on-site in 1998, we got support from many of the Makah people, especially the elders.

Generally speaking, the interests of the species we protect are a priority for us. We protect the interests of our clients. Our clients are not people; they are whales and other marine species that are exploited and exterminated to serve the cultural or economic interests of humans.

Many things have changed because the human population has now reached 7 billion people. All of the red flags have been raised; we are in the process of killing the oceans. In light of that, I find it very difficult to feel any sympathy for a culture, any culture, that is contributing to the destruction of a vulnerable species. And yes, it's true, the Inuit are not to blame for the decline of whale populations, but they could well end up finishing the job. When you get to the bottom of things, people are always to blame. I do not make any distinction between the different groups of humans. The human species is extremely destructive and it has the potential to wipe out the system that makes it possible for people to survive on this earth. And so, I find these stories about traditions to be extremely exasperating; anything that involves killing an endangered species or destroying a natural habitat under the pretext of tradition is unacceptable. Ecology must take precedence over tradition.

It's also very interesting to see that those who claim the traditional right to kill whales or dolphins use methods that are quite far removed from anything that could be seen as "traditional." Modern technology is "enhancing" these "ancestral" customs. In the Faroe Islands, motor boats and jet-skis have now replaced rowboats, while cell phones and sonar have replaced the smoke signals and stones thrown into the water to herd dolphins. A helicopter was even used during a massacre of pilot whales and dolphins in the Faroe Islands in November 2011.

Faroe Islanders enjoy one of the highest standards of living in Europe, so the situation that made killing pilot whales a question of subsistence has long since changed. Today, there is no longer a need for it, yet the killing persists. The massacre of pilot whales in the Faroe Islands is the largest massacre of marine mammals in Europe and goes on in violation of the Berne Convention on the protection of European wildlife and natural habitats, which protects marine mammals. The Faroese argue that they are not part of the European Union, but they do receive large subsidies from Europe by way of Denmark, as the Islands are under the Danish protectorate. Therefore, the EU is in a position to exert economic pressure on the Faroese by making the subsidies conditional on putting an end to the massacres. But once again there is no political will to defend marine life.

These massacres are pure barbarianism, and no tradition can justify the massacre of families and entire groups of sentient, peaceful and socially complex creatures. I have been combating the grind[26] since 1984 and have sent ships to the islands on a number of occasions. In the summer of 2011, we sent two ships and a helicopter, and we also had a team on the ground during July and August, at the height of the hunting season. Between July and August 2010, close to 630 pilot whales were massacred. While we were there, the police ordered that no massacres were to take place within range of our ships. Not one dolphin was killed while we were there. Unfortunately, the killing started up again one week after we left.

During that mission to the Faroe Islands in the summer of 2011, we met with dozens of Faroese. It was quite interesting to hear them condone (for the most part) the massacres that take place in the waters off their islands while condemning the murder of dolphins in Japan, which they refer to as "truly barbaric." Sea Shepherd recently voiced its strong opposition to calls from some surfers living in Reunion to kill sharks after the death of a body boarder. Some of the surfers argued that killing a "few sharks" was not in the least bit shocking, when compared to the slaughter of pilot whales in the Faroe Islands. And yet, the Faroese we spoke with told us that they couldn't understand wanting to kill sharks for the sole purpose of being able to surf without any risk. Japan also talks to us about other massacres that are "much more shocking than our scientific whaling." If we were to listen to that kind of talk, we would never take any action anywhere.

Everyone has some justification for destroying wildlife. Any group that we oppose can become an enemy, but that doesn't bother me very much at all. In fact, my measure of our effectiveness is based on the number of enemies we have. The people we attack who hunt seals, whales and other marine mammals hate us more than any other group that opposes them. There is a fanatical side to their hatred of Sea Shepherd and it sometimes pushes them to do very stupid things in an attempt to stop us. If we were not a serious threat, we would not be effective and we would not be the target of so much aggression. Oscar Wilde once said: "Every effect that one produces gives one an enemy. To be popular one must be a mediocrity." Defending the oceans involves making some noise and telling people things they don't really want to hear. That also means doing things that make people insane with rage.

We know who the enemy is: it is us. We are our own worst enemy, and we are at war with ourselves.

"Human beings are the only animals of which I am thoroughly and cravenly afraid."

— George Bernard Shaw

CHAPTER
23

THE GULAG:
TOO CLOSE FOR
COMFORT

They were putting the whale meat into containers and the smell of fresh meat filled the air. The beach was covered in blood; it was everywhere. The place looked like an open-air abattoir. Flocks of seagulls were flying overhead; they were screeching and throwing themselves at the smallest morsel the women would toss into the sea.

I strongly suspected that the Soviets were violating clause 13B of the International Whaling Commission agreement. A global agreement had authorized the Russians to kill 179 gray whales to in order to meet the subsistence needs of an Aboriginal population of 3,000 people. Prior to 1957, the Aboriginals would kill about forty-five whales. After 1957, the number quickly increased to 200. Some scientists with the International Whaling Commission (IWC) shared my suspicions. We believed that some Soviet entrepreneurs had gotten into the mink business and that they were feeding the animals very cheap protein, namely whale meat. Every year, the application for an on-site investigation by the IWC scientific committee would be rejected by the Russians, who continued to take their quota.

In the summer of 1981, I went to investigate off the Soviet Union's Siberian coast in order to collect proof of the illegal whaling that was going on there.

I left Alaska and passed through the Bering Strait onboard the *Sea Shepherd II* and let the anchor down about a half mile off the Soviet coast. While Bob, Peter Woof and I were headed for the beach in the Zodiac, a feeling came over me of having gotten involved in a time-travel machine; it felt like we were entering another world. From a distance, the beach looked like it was deserted, an eerie place where ghosts might live. Time seemed to have come to a halt on that expanse of sand. As we approached the Lorinc restricted area, I could make out a few silhouettes walking on the beach. They were soldiers, and they were standing on guard with their rifles over their shoulders. I briefed the guys one last time: "Just remember, just act like this is the kind of thing we do every day." We landed on the shell-covered beach about 50 yards from the whaling station. Some Caucasian women were busy using long, sharp knives to cut up the still-fresh whale meat. I expected them to start screaming when they saw us. I imagined they would start shouting something like: "Get lost, you Americans! Stop. Invaders!" But they completely ignored us. They were putting the flesh into containers, and the smell of fresh meat filled the air. The beach was covered in blood; it was everywhere. The place looked like an open-air abattoir. Flocks of seagulls were flying overhead, screeching loudly and throwing themselves at the smallest morsel the women would toss into the sea.

Eric started taking photos so we could bring back some proof that Lorinc was indeed a fur farm. The containers of meat were towed over to a sort of barracks that had been built on the hill. This was, no doubt, where the mink were being housed; I could see the cages stacked on top of each other. The whale meat was being used as a cheap source of food, which made it possible to maximize the profits from the fur business. We had a good understanding of why the Russians would not authorize the IWC inspectors to visit the site. The scene hardly coincided with the traditional ancestral hunt invoked by the Russian delegation. Eric was taking photo after photo and filming at the same time. We would have more than enough proof to bring back.

Bob pulled me back to reality: "Paul, look. There could be some trouble." The two soldiers who were standing on guard were coming toward us. They were in no hurry, barely looking at us. We took a few more photos, pretending to be unaware of them. Then we slowly headed back toward the Zodiac, trying to look as nonchalant as possible. The soldiers looked very young; one of them was wearing a uniform that was much too big for him. They hadn't reported our presence to their base; everything was still okay. I decided to take advantage of the situation to get back into the Zodiac so we could land on a beach on the other side. As we followed along the shoreline, Eric continued to photograph the women cutting up the meat. The soldiers did an about-face, but didn't seem alarmed. Our orange suits gave us a team-like appearance; the soldiers had no doubt assumed that we were a group of Russian scientists or technicians.

We came ashore once again to take more photos of the farm. Shortly after that, the soldiers started coming toward us. They were walking a little more quickly, and this time it was impossible to pretend that we hadn't seen them. They were wearing khaki-colored caps, and I couldn't take my eyes off the red star. The larger of the two spoke to me. I had taken one semester of Russian language courses at university. It was finally going to be of some use to me: "*Shto eta?*"[27] he asked me. "*Eto Zodiac,*" I replied, smiling. He was not smiling at all. He stared at the boat, his eyes were bulging and he looked furious. Stupefied, he came up to me and screamed out: "*Niet, eta Mercury! Eta American!*" I put on a big ear-to-ear grin that instinctively made him step up and grab his gun. His companion did likewise. It was easy to see what they were thinking; alarm bells were going off in their heads. It had just dawned on them that they were now face to face with ... the Enemy.

The two soldiers no doubt expected to see us draw weapons, because they ran off to take shelter behind some boats that were lying abandoned on the beach. Seeing that we were still standing there with our arms at our sides, one of them shouted out something from their hiding place. Trying to mask the fact that I was nervous, I pointed to the big ship from which we had come and that was waiting for us just off the coast. The soldier pointed the barrel of his weapon at my back while we got into the Zodiac as calmly as possible. I told the guys to keep smiling and to wave at them. I looked straight ahead and asked Eric to keep me informed about what was happening on the shore while continuing to make friendly gestures. I was counting on the soldiers' hesitation to give us the time to make our getaway; I was hoping that they were afraid. I reassured myself: if they were crack shots, they probably would not have been sent to patrol this isolated beach in the middle of Siberia. "The first soldier has his weapon aimed at us and the other guy is loading his," Eric said nervously. Were they going to shoot at unarmed men who were smiling and waving at them? "Let's give ourselves up, because these guys are obviously going to shoot at us!" "That's out of the question because if we do, all of this will have been for nothing. If they shoot at us, they have an international situation on their hands. We'll just keep going," I said.

We kept going in the Zodiac, but the shoreline behind us was taking a long time to disappear and the distance that separated us from the *Sea Shepherd II* seemed infinite. Each yard felt like a mile, and each second lasted for an hour. With a sigh of relief, Bob announced that they were putting down their guns. They were now running toward the hill; we were sure they would report the incident to their base. At long last, we boarded the *Sea Shepherd II*. And we had the proof that we had come here to get our hands on.

Marly Jones, one of the crew, wanted to get out of there right away. But I said: "We are not done here just yet. We still have to locate the *Zevezdny*." That was the name of the whaling ship that was carrying out the so-called Aboriginal hunt. The purpose of the expedition was two-fold. On the one hand, we wanted to bring back proof that the hunt was illegal. But we also wanted to render the *Zevezdny* harmless. Marly couldn't believe his ears: "You must be completely insane. I demand that we all vote on this because you are going to get us all killed!" I simply replied: "Sorry, Marly, but the day when this ship becomes a democracy, you'll be the first to know." Then I turned to the officers: "Okay, that's enough chit-chat, let's go track down these bastards!" We headed south and followed the coastline.

A Russian cruiser headed toward us. The soldiers on the beach had, in fact, alerted them. Fifteen minutes after we raised the anchor, two Soviet combat helicopters were flying over the ship. We could see the red stars on their flanks, and the barrels of the guns were pointed right at us. I told the crew to ignore them. A few seconds later, the helicopters were firing flares onto the deck. The crew quickly threw them overboard. The radar was indicating that there was another vessel behind us. Using the binoculars, I was able to make out a military vessel that was coming toward us at high speed. So I decided to change direction and head for American waters. We had stirred up a real hornet's nest.

We were about 35 miles from the dividing line between Russian and American waters. I calculated the speed the Russian vessel was doing; it was coming toward us at 30 knots, and we were barely doing 15. They would catch up with us within 30 minutes and we would still be in Russian waters. I quickly thought of a plan that would help us gain some time. I asked the crew to smear the rail with grease, prepare the water cannons and put on their gas masks. In addition to the flag that was flying over the stern of the ship, I hoisted the Russian courtesy flag on the port side and the United Nations flag on the starboard side. The Russian cruiser was getting closer, and we could read the name on the hull: *Kommunist*. The captain of the civilian vessel was waiting for the military ship. The helicopters still hovered overhead, making a deafening noise. The military ship would soon arrive. It bore the name *Iceberg*, and the number 024 was painted in white on its gray hull. There were machine guns on both sides of the deck and a helipad in the stern.

The ship pulled up alongside us about 50 yards off our port side. The soldiers onboard were all armed with automatic weapons. The captain was sitting up on the bridge, about 15 feet over our heads, looking down at us. I began to doubt our chances of getting out of this one because this particular iceberg was a fire-breathing one. Compared to our old rust bucket, the military vessel looked like it had traveled back in time, from the future. It was as if two machines from different eras found themselves occupying the same dimension. It hoisted its flag to order us to halt. Marc, one of the officers, asked me what he should do. We were only about 10 miles from American waters. "We are not going to stop now," I said. On the deck, some of the crew were getting nervous. Leslie Fillebrown burst onto the bridge, despite the fact that it was against the rules: "What are you doing? We have to stop! They'll sink our boat! Someone needs to stop this ship." She was crying and pointing her finger at me: "He's crazy. He's completely insane!"

"Perhaps you'd prefer to take up permanent residence in Siberia, Leslie. Marc, get her out of here and lock the door behind you," I shot back. "Yes, captain. My pleasure!" Marc answered.

For close to ten minutes, the ships navigated side by side. The crews stared each other down, and nobody blinked. Clearly, the Russians weren't sure what to do with us. The warship was impressive; it looked like a steel-clad monster that had surged up out of the depths, preparing to devour us. "They are flashing their lights at us, telling us to stop. Should we stop?" Marc asked timidly. I answered: "Listen, Marc, if we let these guys come onboard, they will confiscate the vessel and we will end our days at the end of a chain, shovel in hand in a salt mine. OK?"

Suddenly, we heard the crackle of the VHF. Someone was saying, in very bad English: "*Sea Shepherd. Sea Shepherd.* You must shut off your engines." Feeling somewhat blasé, I grabbed the microphone and came back with: "Stop killing whales." After a moment of silence, the voice was back: "*Sea Shepherd.* Turn off your engines. The Soviet Union is going to board your vessel." "Sorry, but I don't have enough room onboard for the Soviet Union," I replied, stifling a snicker. But the captain was not laughing. "Turn off your engines immediately! You are violating the laws of the Soviet Union. You are under arrest. That's an order!"

Marc turned to me and said: "I guess that's it. It's all over now. Should we shut down the engines, Paul?" I replied: "Marc, I am sure that they will not arrest us. I have already lost one boat to this kind of game, and I am not going to lose another." Marc looked quite alarmed: "But, what if they start shooting at us?" "Then, they will have an international incident on their hands that will draw attention to their whale hunt. They don't want that kind of publicity. They will not shoot." The voice started in again: "*Sea Shepherd*, you are under arrest." Growing tired of all this, I grabbed the microphone: "You are violating the laws of the IWC. Your country is illegally killing whales, and we have already sent the proof on to the United States. I am not authorizing you to board our vessel and we have no intention of stopping. We do not recognize the authority of a pirate nation that poaches whales."

The Russians did not respond, but they did increase their speed and cut across our bow. The men in the stern of the Russian ship were getting a heavy cable ready to throw in the path of our propeller, in the hopes of disabling it. We passed right over it, without any problems. I took up the microphone again: "Captain, our boat is equipped with a ducted propeller so that maneuver won't work on us." The captain did not reply. He just increased his speed again in order to cut in front of us so he could block our route. I shouted into the microphone: "Captain, your vessel is worth millions of dollars; mine is not worth very much. Get out of our way or I will ram you. I will not stop. I repeat, I will not stop." The gap that separated us was quickly disappearing. Marc was at the wheel, and he was livid: "For God's sake, Captain. If we get into a collision with them, I'll never see Melbourne again." "Do not change the heading, not even by one degree," I told him. "If we show even the slightest sign of weakness, we are done for. I am not bluffing. If he doesn't move, we're going to ram him." I picked up the microphone again, and this time I wanted to speak to the crew: "Brace yourselves and have your life jackets on hand." The ball was in the Russian captain's court. He had to believe that I was crazy enough to do it in order to understand that I was not bluffing. He would have to answer to his superior for the damage to his nice shiny ship, so it was better for him to avoid any mistakes.

If we survived the shock, we would still have to make a run for it. It was still possible to do it — the *Sea Shepherd II* had enough power for that. If we rammed the military ship doing 15 knots, we could do some serious damage. Our boat had a high, pointed prow, perfect for a "bottle opener" maneuver. And because they had a water ingress on the side, a damaged bow would make it harder for their vessel to stay afloat than it would be for ours. Of course, the helicopters were still flying overhead, but, in the general confusion, we might be able to get away. Just when a collision seemed inevitable, the destroyer changed its heading and let us pass about 50 yards behind its prow. I could only imagine the captain's fury. The *Kommunist* moved in closer and the *Iceberg* took up its position on our port side once again. There were barely 20 yards between us when the soldiers started taking the coverings off the guns on the upper deck. I shouted out to the crew to tell them to keep smiling and waving. It was the only option we had left; we could only hope that our friendly demeanor would confuse them. We prayed that we would make it out alive. I left the bridge to keep an eye on the Russians; the soldiers were loading the machine guns. They were waiting for orders; the moment of truth was approaching. I was expecting the Russians to spray the deck with gunfire before boarding us. It seemed like the end was at hand ...

And then, something miraculous happened. If there had not been so many witnesses on that day, I would not have dared to tell the story because nobody would have believed me. The crew started screaming all at once; but they were crying out with joy. I thought they had lost their minds. But the Russians were standing motionless. In the narrow space that separated the *Iceberg* from the *Sea Shepherd II*, a geyser shot up out of the water onto the decks of both ships. In a flash, the Russians disappeared in the foamy spray. We had no idea what was happening and neither did they. An enormous California gray whale had just surfaced between the two boats. It remained motionless for a few moments, breathing peacefully in the churned-up waters. Then it disappeared into the deep in a swirl of foam. The Russians instinctively veered to port and Marc veered to starboard. The gap between us was now much larger.

A whale ... A whale had surged up from out of the depths of the ocean to distance us from the Russian machine guns. Everyone who witnessed this magical episode could not help but think that something mystical happened on that day. Something that goes beyond Cartesian logic. A few years before that, a man who knew more about whales than I will ever know had told me that I could count on them if I was courageous enough to go to sea to defend them: "The whales will be there when you need them. You can be sure that they will be there for you," Paul Spong had promised me.

Eric burst out onto the deck: "Good God! Did you see that!? That was incredible!" I was silent. We were putting distance between ourselves and the Russians. All of a sudden, the helicopters turned back. Their incessant buzzing disappeared and was replaced by a calming silence. On the radar, we spotted land. It was St. Lawrence Island. I did a few calculations, then made an announcement: "Ladies and Gentlemen, we are now entering American waters!" On that day, a whale had guided the whale shepherds through the valley of darkness.

"The extermination of sharks is one of the biggest ecological time bombs ever triggered by humanity."
— Dr. Erich Ritter

CHAPTER
24

THE
KILLER SHARK
MYTH

The oceans provide us with 80% of the oxygen we breathe. The ocean ecosystem is made up of food chains that are closely interrelated. Sharks are at the top of the entire system; they are what scientists refer to as "keystone species," which means that their disappearance would cause the entire system to collapse.

Hollywood has transformed them into blood-thirsty monsters, and in our collective imagination, they are images from the movie *Jaws*. Sharks are paying a heavy price for the success of Spielberg's film ... On average, five people per year die as a result of a shark attack. And at the same time, humans kill between 75 and 100 million of them under conditions that are unimaginable for any other creature. And yet, in our eyes, they are the monsters.

Shark attacks are extremely rare. On a planet populated by some 7 billion people, several hundred million of whom are in daily contact with the sea, only five people per year, on average, die as a result of a shark attack. And these incidents are, generally speaking, the result of a "error" on the part of the shark. They do not target people intentionally; they do not even like us, and we probably don't taste very good. More human deaths can be attributed to soft drink vending machines, coconuts, and drownings that occur in swimming pools. More golfers are struck and killed by lightning each year, and that fact doesn't create any hysteria. Yes, playing golf is more dangerous than swimming with sharks ... More people are killed by bees, elephants and ostriches, and we don't think of those creatures as monsters. But sharks are monsters in our eyes, and that's how we justify massacring them.

Sharks can be compared to lightning. They are an unpredictable force of nature, but both can be avoided by taking a few simple and intelligent precautions. That being said, surfing or diving with sharks is less dangerous than driving your car to the beach to go surfing. Every year, 50,000 people die on the highways in the United States alone, but it would never occur to us to stop using our cars.

If we look at sharks in a different light and if we get beyond the image of a vicious creature that lurks in the darkest corners of our worst nightmares, the image that was created by mass culture horror films, we would see humans are the real monsters. We pitilessly massacre more than 75 million sharks every year so that we can make shark fin soup, fish and chips, snake oil — or just for the fun of it — all due to fear and ignorance.

Everything I used to know about sharks I learned by watching *Jaws*. Images from the film stayed with me when I went diving with the great whites off South Africa. But when I actually came face to face with them, my fear gave way to another feeling, one that I was not in the least expecting to feel: admiration. In the water, just a few yards away from me, they were not aggressive or furious; they were simply serene and beautiful. Five magnificent great whites were gliding gracefully by, right before my eyes. I had never felt so comfortable and so humbled in the wilds of nature. Nor did I have any idea that I was going to feel that way. Sharks have been around since before the time of the dinosaurs, and you can really see the kind of perfection nature is capable of creating when it has that much time at its disposal. They are the incarnation of absolute perfection. I was expecting to find myself in the water alongside a monster, but that didn't happen. Instead, I had an encounter with the most majestic creature that I have ever seen. But that moment of pure magic was tainted with a bittersweet aftertaste, because we are in the process of exterminating them and yet we are more or less indifferent about it.

There are more Bengal tigers in the world than there are great whites, and yet all attempts to have the great white protected have failed. Sharks cannot survive the war that humanity is waging against them. For the most part, sharks are timid creatures; they reach sexual maturity relatively late and give birth to very few young over the course of a lifetime. They will not be able to withstand what we are inflicting on them.

Sharks have come to be synonymous with death. But, ironically enough, they are essential to life in the oceans. And as you know, our survival depends on the survival of the oceans.

Sharks have been shaping evolution in the oceans for 550 million years (the average lifespan of a species is usually about one million years). The speed, behavior, camouflage and other features of every species of fish in the sea has developed because of the presence of sharks. Being at the top of the food chain, sharks have pointed evolution in a certain direction. If the sharks were to disappear, all of that cohesion would disintegrate and there would be repercussions for all forms of marine life.

The oceans provide us with 80% of the oxygen we breathe, so they are a vital planetary system. Sharks play an essential role in the health of our oceans and if they disappear, the consequences for the marine ecosystem would be disastrous. The ocean ecosystem is made up of food chains that are closely interrelated. Sharks are at the top of the entire system; they are what scientists refer to as "keystone species," which means that their disappearance would cause the entire system to collapse. For that reason, decapitating the ocean's food network could bring about the end of a number of other species. Exterminating the shark is no doubt one of the biggest ecological time bombs ever triggered by humanity.

Eighteen species of sharks have already been included on the International Union for the Conservation of Nature (IUCN) endangered species list. But none of them is fully protected. And contrary to popular opinion, Asia is not the only guilty party. Europe is responsible for one third of shark fin exports to Hong Kong. And in France, shark products are being sold at nearly all of the "sustainable development" fairs. France is also the country that kills the second highest number of sharks in Europe, Spain being at the top of that list. So much work remains to be done, but we are racing against the clock because it has been estimated that in the next twenty years, sharks could disappear completely.

The implementation of an international moratorium on the shark trade, similar to the whale moratorium currently in place, could still save them. A handful of jurisdictions, including French Polynesia, Israel, Hawaii, Congo-Brazzaville and Honduras, have introduced a moratorium on the shark fishery within their territorial waters. But given that a bowl of shark fin soup sells for between $50 and $400, it will be difficult to convince other jurisdictions to do the same.

Since 2000, we have been working in the Galápagos Islands, trying to keep poachers out of the Marine Reserve. If we cannot put an end to the massacre of sharks in the Galápagos, it cannot be done anywhere else. In 2011, we installed an AIS (automatic identification system) surveillance system at a cost of about $1.3 million. It is used to monitor all of the comings and goings inside the reserve, and we are also working in close collaboration with the Ecuadorian national police force. To date, we have confiscated about 200,000 shark fins. And we are currently in the process of expanding our shark campaign to other parts of the world. Protecting sharks is an absolute priority.

It's true that Sea Shepherd is better known for its whale or seal campaigns. But it also conducts campaigns on behalf of other less popular species such as sharks, and less charismatic species such as sea cucumbers.

We are working to protect all marine species, regardless of how cute they are or are not. I'm talking about everything from zooplankton to large whales. It is much more difficult to garner media attention and raise funds to launch a sea cucumber campaign, but we do it just the same. We do not make a distinction between the different marine species. They all deserve to be protected whether or not they meet our anthropocentric criteria for beauty or not.

"Free man, you will always cherish the sea!"
— Charles Baudelaire

EPILOGUE

The problem with our economic and political systems is that they focus on the short term and not on the long-term consequences of our actions. But all over the world there are people working to make the world a better place and to make the ecology movement what it is. And we have come a long way.

W hat do you think the future holds for the whales, the oceans and the planet in general?

The situation is easy enough to understand. If the oceans die, we will die. Humanity doesn't seem to have the slightest idea of the severity of the threats facing our oceans. Since 1950, there has been a 30% reduction in the amount of oxygen produced by phytoplankton. Why? Because of plastic pollution, oil pollution, heavy metals, acidification, the spread of dead zones, climate change, the destruction of estuaries, overfishing, bottom trawling, long lines, drift nets, dynamite fishing, whaling, sealing, the destruction of corals, aquaculture, drilling into the seabed in search of oil or minerals and many other factors introduced by humans.

The future of the oceans is our future. If we want to have a future, we must protect life in the oceans. The other option is to allow our colossal ignorance and speciesist arrogance to result in the collective suicide of our species, which from an evolutionary perspective will not have shined its light on this planet for a very long time.

It is already getting late. But perhaps there is still time to bring the oceans back to life because I am convinced that the impossible is possible. In 1962, the year he was sent to prison, the very idea that Nelson Mandela could one day become the President of South Africa was unthinkable and seemed thoroughly impossible. But it happened. The answers to our problems are out there. It's up to us to find them. In this struggle, there is no room for self pity and we cannot afford the luxury of pessimism. Courageous, imaginative and passionate people can turn the impossible into the possible. Those people are you, me and anyone who has the desire to change things

But one question keeps popping up: "What can be done to make the world a better place?"

We can start by refraining from eating everything in the ocean, because there is no such thing as a sustainable fishery on a planet populated by 7 billion people.

And individual people can make a difference. Each one of us can contribute something to changing the world. We simply need to become aware of our power. Unfortunately, our society gives us the message that in order to change the world we just need to vote, or sign a petition, etc. We are not used to the idea of people getting directly involved and taking matters into their own hands. And there are many different ways to do that. For example, in 1979, one of my crew members, who was 19 years old at the time, was Alex Pacheco. One year later, he founded People for the Ethical Treatment of Animals. Today, PETA is one of the largest animal rights organizations in the world. Many people have launched their own nature conservation projects after having spent time in the ranks of Sea Shepherd: protection of corals, turtles, sharks, etc. I think it changes people's lives somewhat.

The important thing is for each one of us to do what we can, in our own way. We should always remember that. We should all put our own talents to work to make the world a better place. It doesn't matter if you're a lawyer, a writer, a teacher, an actor, a journalist, an architect, a nurse or anything else, as long as you always ask yourself what the future consequences of your actions will be. According to the philosophy of the Iroquois Nation: "Never do anything without thinking about the consequences it will have seven generations later." Merely adopting that philosophy will make an enormous difference.

The problem with our economic and political systems is that they focus on the short term: short-term investments for short-term gains. There is not much of a focus on the long-term consequences of our actions. But all over the world there are people and small organizations that are working to make the world a better place and to make the ecology movement what it is. And we have come a long way. In 1972, we set up a giant banner in Vancouver; it bore the message "Ecology" in giant yellow letters, and below that: "Get informed and get involved ..." Nobody knew what the word "ecology" meant. In 1980, if you told someone you were a vegan, they might have thought you were from the planet Vega. Nobody knew what it meant. We have come a long way.

Are you the same person as that little boy who used to save animals in an Eastern Canadian fishing village?

I am still the same person. I became an activist at the age of 11, when I started disarming the traps set by hunters in New Brunswick and Maine. Back then, I was freeing the beavers and destroying the traps. I am still doing the work I started doing a half century ago in the woods around Passamaquoddy Bay, but today I am doing it at sea.

People sometimes thank you for the "sacrifices" you make. But when I look at you, I don't see someone who is making sacrifices, I see one of the happiest people I know.

I chose the right path, the one that gave me no choice but to choose it. When I look back, I see a life of satisfaction over the course of which I was able to accomplish most of the things I wanted to do. And I'm still doing that today. I've also got an adorable and intelligent daughter. I didn't have to sacrifice my family in order to make my dreams come true, and I didn't have to give up my dreams in order to have a family. Today, my daughter is pursuing her own dreams and she is involved with Sea Shepherd.

It has always been my dream to defend the oceans and marine life. And I have done it to the best of my ability, using the limited resources at my disposal, and I will continue to do it until the day I die.

What is your wish for the oceans?

I would like to see an international oceans policy put in place. If such a policy existed, Sea Shepherd would not need to get involved. We already have all the laws and treaties we need to protect the oceans. The problem is the lack of political and economic will to enforce them. If that job was given to some international body or other, that would be a huge step toward protecting the oceans.

What is your recipe for happiness?

I have always lived my life by following my heart and I have never focused on money or status. I never worked one day in my life for the sole purpose of making money. I have always valued freedom over financial security. So many people tell me that they would like to do what I do, but they say they can't because they have debts to pay back, bills to pay, a retirement to save for or a family to raise.

When I was 20 years old, I thought that thinking about your retirement was akin to giving yourself up for dead, and I rejected the idea of saving for that. I'm 60 years old now and I still feel the same way. Life should be spent living instead of anticipating the end. As for money, over the years I have come to learn that when you follow the dictates of your heart, money will be there. Enough money, in any case, to meet your needs and sometimes even a little more, and that makes it possible to be generous and to bring forth other ideas.

Experience has taught me that the secret to happiness is detachment from material desires, a focus on the desires of the heart and a curious mind, regardless of what people might think. Happiness is not about what you own, it's about what's in your heart, the things you try and what you do to make the world a better place, regardless of how you choose to get involved.

Living outside the material world doesn't mean lacking material assets. It means not being possessed by the things you possess. It means not being terrified of losing your material assets, if it becomes necessary, and it also means not betraying your integrity, your principles and especially your freedom in order to keep them. It means refraining from making decisions that are motivated by profit. It means making your dreams come true, whatever they may be.

NOTES

1. Adopted in the emotional aftermath of the 9-11 terrorist attacks, it gives US federal agencies extraordinary powers to enter private homes, seize documents and bug telephone lines, without requiring that the legal protocols in force be respected.

2. According to a 2005 United Nations report

3. The sixth mass extinction crisis was described by the paleoanthropologist Richard Leakey.

4. In the documentary *Battleship Antarctica*, 2007.

5. The Foundation Series.

6. United Nations World Charter for Nature (Sections 21 to 24), U.N.Doc. A/37/51, 1982.

7. Orenthal James Simpson is the former American professional football player and actor known for having been accused of murdering his ex-wife and her companion.

8. A survey published in *A la recherche du nouvel ennemi* [In Search of the New Enemy], Éditions L'Échapée, 2009.

9. Note from Lamya E.: We contacted the TV channel at the time to obtain information about the show in order to file a defamation complaint, but it got back to us the day after the three-month deadline for initiating defamation proceedings had expired.

10. In January of 2011, Tokyo announced that the whaling fleet would be leaving the sanctuary in the Antarctic due to being harassed by the Sea Shepherd crews.

11. These figures correspond to the whales that the whaling fleet was not able to kill in order to reach its self-imposed quota of 980 whales per season.

12. TV series that tells the story of the Sea Shepherd missions in Antarctica. It airs on the Animal Planet channel.

13. The Food and Agriculture Organization of the United Nations (FAO) has forecasted a world-wide collapse of commercial fisheries by 2048.

14. Estimate from the FAO.

15. *After the Tsunami: Rapid Environmental Assessment*, UNEP, 2005, p. 126 –37.

16. William Wilberforce (1759 –1833) spent his entire life fighting to have slavery abolished in England. He won that battle a short time before his death.

17. Frederick Douglass (1818–1895) was an American politician and writer. Born a slave, he became one of the most famous 19th-century abolitionists.

18. Susan Brownell Anthony (1820–1906) was a civil rights activist who played a pivotal role in the women's suffrage movement in the United States. For over 45 years, she traveled throughout the US and Europe and gave between 75 and 100 speeches per year on the topic of women's rights. On November 5, 1872, President Grant was re-elected for a second term; Susan B. Anthony was arrested and sentenced for attempting to cast a ballot.

19. Aung San Suu Kyi was born in 1945 in Rangoon. She is a Burmese politician and leader of the non-violent opposition to the military dictatorship in power in her country.

20. The vegan diet excludes all animal products and by-products.

21. According to data from the FAO and the World Bank, the amount of fishing subsidies, which have a direct influence on fishing capacity and provide fodder for overfishing, amounted to $10 billion in 2000. Close to 80% of all global subsidies were given out by developed countries. The report was published by the United Nations Department of Information, DPI/2556D, May 2010.

22. In fact, as stipulated in Senate Resolution 33: "Given that hooded seals are an essential component in the complex ecosystem of the North West Atlantic and because seals consume predators of cod, removing the seals could prevent the recovery of the cod stocks."

23. Article written by freelance journalist Caroline Muscat. Published by fish2fork. com on June 28, 2010.

24. The figure is based on an estimated average tuna size of about 100 kg, and the size is getting smaller and smaller with each passing year.

25. *Mind the Gap: An Analysis of the Mediterranean Bluefin Trade*, Pew Environment Group, 2011.

26. Abbreviation of the Faroese name for the pilot whale massacres.

27. "What is it ?
   -It's a Zodiac.
   -No it's not; it's a Mercury! It's American!"

INDEX

Page numbers in **boldface** refer to photo captions